PUPPY TRAINING MADE EASY

A Step-By-Step Guide to Prep Your Home, Teach Basic Commands, and Create a Lifelong Bond with Dogs of All Personalities

---

F&F PUBLICATIONS

Contents

Disclaimer Warning

The content of this book should not be regarded as medical
advice in any capacity. If your dog appears unwell, or you
have any questions or concerns about their behavior or wellbeing, it is the recommendation of the author and all involved
parties that your dog is tended to by a registered and
recognized veterinarian.

Introduction

Do you remember the first dog your family had when you were still a kid? The memories I have of our first dogs are nothing but good. When I ask my parents about these dogs, they sing a bit of a different tune. I remember the playing and the laughing, the boundless energy and the companionship. My parents remember the destroyed shoes, broken toys, ruined rugs, and that non-stop barking that made them wish they had never given the neighbors our number.

I think this perfectly sums up dog ownership. However, with the proper training method for your new furry friend, you can overcome some of these main challenges that you will face as a new puppy owner. Let's better your chances of creating the perfect companion who will fit in with your family almost as if they were always meant to be there. We will accomplish this through what is called The Puppy Prodigy Method.

Of course, owning a dog comes with some challenges. You need to ensure that your new family member is properly socialized. They need to be able to interact with other dogs and behave themselves in a socially acceptable way. Just like humans they also need to have regular medical check-ups, and unlike humans, they require a lot more regular vaccinations. Then you still need to teach them how to use the bathroom correctly and to be comfortable in their crates, just like a baby needs to learn to sleep in their own room eventually. Another similarity between babies and puppies is that they will eventually put anything they can find into their mouths. This means they will also need to be taught what they are allowed to sink their teeth in, and what they should avoid.

Yes, I know that these challenges might sound like a lot to the first-time dog owner. Fear not, this guide will help you to over-come them quite easily. Plus, the rewards from having a dog join your family will make this journey through overcoming the challenges worth it.

It is rare to find unconditional love. Well, maybe not as rare as we might think. When you welcome a four-legged angel into your family, you are guaranteed to be on the receiving end of unconditional love. If that's not enough to convince you, how about some health benefits? Yes, dogs have been linked to reduced stress levels, lower blood pressure, and reduced risk of heart disease. They also help you to get in some more physical exercise. Whether it's from walking your new companion or playing a game of fetch with them. Of course, having a puppy at your side also immediately makes you more approachable to others. I cannot begin to put a number on the people whom I've

had pleasant conversations with, just because they wanted to greet my furry friend. The benefits don't stop there either. Puppies can even be a powerful parenting tool. There is no better way to teach your child the true meaning of responsibility and compassion while ensuring that they have a smile on their face the entire time.

We'll start our journey off by identifying the different personalities that your companion might have. This is quite important as it will have a big impact on the approach you take to training your puppy. It is important to remember that every breed has its own personality, and within each breed, each puppy will have their own distinct personality as well. There are so many possibilities that I would probably be able to write a book on each different breed. This book is a general guide to help make your training endeavors easier, which means that we'll be taking a broad approach while giving you the tools to personalize the approach to your companion's own personality.

Of course, there is a bit of preparation to be done before you even welcome your puppy into your home. But don't worry, I've got you covered there as well. Through years of experience, and countless hours of research I guarantee you that I've thought about nearly everything that you need to do to make sure your home is ready to welcome in the new addition, without the usual stress-inducing chaos.

I will give you the tools to ensure that once your puppy is welcomed into this loving home of yours, and you have identified their personality you can also impart on them the skills needed to ensure that they are both safe and obedient in any situ-

ation. Whether you are out for a jog, visiting the beach, at the dog park, or just need to find a reason to be in the yard so you can get a bit of fresh air.

Usually, when people hear the word obedience, they think that it is impossible to have a strong and positive bond with the puppy while still having it be obedient to them. This is not true. To ensure that you and your furry companion both enjoy each other's company and love I'll show you how to use positive reinforcement. Without a doubt, you'll be their favorite human in no time!

Just like humans, however, your puppy will need their own space. While they may not be able to have their very own bedroom as we do, a crate can create a safe space for them where they will feel comfortable retreating to whenever they feel stressed, or just tired in general. You'll learn how to help them feel more comfortable in their own space, as well as how to set up a crate so that it fully accommodates all their needs.

There are quite a few behavioral issues that are common for dogs. Basic training will help to keep these issues under control, but there are others that might pop up over time as a result of a variety of influences outside of your control. To help you be prepared for these issues when they arise, and to ensure that you are able to prevent these issues from creating problems down the road, we'll look into them and equip you with the practical solutions that you will need.

Lastly, a dog is a family companion. While, yes, they tend to be close to one person in the family, they are still there to be a part of the family and bring joy to everyone. This is why it is so

important that your dog has a strong and positive bond with each family member, and that everyone is united and consistent when it comes to the little furball's training.

Before I became so well-versed in puppy training, I faced the same problems that so many other first-time dog owners face. Without the experience or knowledge that is contained in these pages, it is difficult to understand your puppy's behavior and even their needs to a point. I was inconsistent in the approach I took to training my pup and had no idea that there were different methods to use. This, of course, encouraged more behavioral problems than it solved. But I learned. It took a lot of time for me to do the research, go through the courses, and even more time to build up the experience. Now that I have it, I want to help as many people as I can to experience the ease of finding, training, and bonding with a loving furry friend. This is why these pages are filled with everything I have learned and in your hands.

But enough about me now, let's jump in and start to take the first steps towards a happier home for you, and your newest fluffball of love.

himself that everyday life is a miracle and worth bread with ... simple fragments, and that everyone is blessed in a moment when ... come to that bad, that it's value."

... so I decide to walk myself in my appointment, I need ... ... neighbors, and so many other features. Dog owners, too ... ... obtain the experience ... in which ... that I won mind to rescue ... pets. It is difficult ... their ... your puppy's behavior and ... even their needs to a point was to ensure that the approach ... ... of using my dog had had learning, take that there were ... different medicine so that ... this ... of course ... resources is once ... ... that I ... at it ... a time ... ... out to trade the insight so that I learn like I can expand over ... ... harvest from ... the experience ... view that harvest I want ... ... is mine nature ... ... to experience the case of ... ... bonfire ... ... leaving my ... friend. This is all ... ... once when ... with everything ... I have learned and what ... finds.

But remember about me now, looking around, and start to take it often ... ... with a happier home for you, and ... ... turned at me.

ONE

Puppy Personality Profiling

Dogs each have their own completely unique personality just like humans do. Yes, it is true that each breed tends to share more similar traits. For example, Jack Russells tend to be more energetic and playful than Chihuahuas. This does not mean that you won't find a lazy Jack Russell, you are just more likely to find them being energetic. In fact, actual studies (Chopik & Weaver, 2019) have found that the personality traits of the owner transfer into the personality of the dog. In other words, yes, dogs share personality traits with their owners.

Introduction to The Importance of Understanding Your Puppy's Unique Personality

Personalities are not set in stone. They can and will change over time. So, while you might fall in love with the personality of a puppy at the start, when they spend time with you and start to take on more of your personality traits, that original personality

will change quite a bit. I want to take a moment and remind you that this is a good thing. Your pup will adopt a personality that is shared by your household, which will allow them to fit in with your family. Identifying their unique personality will have a big impact on the approach you take to their training. We'll take a closer look at how personalities impact training techniques later on. For now, let's just identify each type of personality.

The Confident Puppy

These are the pups that might appear fearless. They will go up to any other dog, human, or most animals for that matter. This confidence will often establish these puppies as the ringleaders of other dogs. These pups socialize easily and tend to display their personalities more prominently than other pups do.

This might make them sound like the perfect dog. However, have you ever met someone so confident that they become arrogant? How does that usually end for them? When this happens in dogs, the confident puppy will often use aggression to maintain their place as the leader and to show off their confidence. Almost like the stereotypical high school jock.

There's a common misconception that when a dog uses this aggression to maintain their role, this is just the natural order of things. Wolves do it all the time, right? Well while your pup might be related to wolves, dogs are no longer wolves. Unless your dog is being actively trained to be a working security dog, there is no good reason for them to participate in this aggressive behavior. Even then, aggression towards other dogs is discouraged.

These pups will need a lot more positive reinforcement and should start training as soon as possible to help ensure their confidence does not get the better of them.

The Free Spirited Puppy

When we talk about a free-spirited pup, I want you to think of that one person in school who didn't fit in with any group. When someone tried to force them into an uncomfortable social environment, they didn't hide their disinterest. When they were left to do and go wherever they wanted, they would be able to do so without needing much supervision or guidance. These free-spirited puppies are the same.

They tend to be independent and great at looking after themselves. This independence, however, will mean that it is more difficult for them to socialize with other animals and humans. When they are forced into these social interactions, they may become aggressive towards the stranger, or even the person forcing them into these situations. While they might be able to accept others after a while, these puppies are more likely to only bond with one human for their entire life. That human, will of course enjoy their love and loyalty in a way that nobody else will ever be privileged to.

While free-spirited pups may pick up on their training quite quickly thanks to the bond they create with their human, you will need to give extra focus to socializing these pups and making them more comfortable in social settings, in order to ensure that they do not become anti-social.

The Laidback Puppy

To continue our comparison of high school personalities, the laidback puppy is that one kid who seems to just drift through life and makes friends with everyone. Yet they tend not to put too much weight on things like their schoolwork or the situation that they find themselves in. These puppies are the same. They will always be ready to play and have fun, and love to meet new people, other animals, and objects.

This is where the downside of laidback puppies comes in. They enjoy everything new so much that they often get way too excited and end up bumping into people and objects with little regard for whether it is appropriate, they are hurting someone, or causing damage to objects.

This care-free attitude will mean that you need to begin training your laidback puppy as soon as possible, be more dedicated to their regular and consistent training, and have a lot more patience with these puppies than with most other personality types. While this all may sound extremely negative, I don't want you to worry. With these puppies, you will often find yourself having to hold back laughter at their antics while trying to get your little goofball to focus on their training.

The Adaptable Puppy

Adaptable puppies are those kids in school who just seem to be good at everything. Teachers love them, the jocks don't bully them, and the rest of the school has no issue with them. These puppies are a lot like laidback puppies in the sense that they tend

to socialize just as easily, but they are also easier to train. They have much better control over their emotions and don't tend to get overexcited.

While these puppies do sound like a dream to train, you should keep in mind that they can accidentally be taught negative behavior just as easily as the positive behavior that you want them to learn. So, you need to be a lot more strict with yourself when it comes to their training, how you interact with them, and when you praise and reward them.

The Sweet Natured Puppy

These are the teacher's pets. They live to please and get their gratification from seeing you happy. They will pick up on training quite easily once they see that this pleases you and they will enjoy your showers of love and affection so much that they tend to stay near you instead of going off to explore or play with other animals. Sweet-natured pups tend to be less aggressive than any other personality type and will much rather hide behind your legs or in your arms than get involved in conflict.

While these pups will also pick training up quite easily, you will need to not only socialize them to show them that other humans and animals are in fact okay to be around, but you will also need to train them to respond to you while they are in social environments. Sweet-natured pups tend to focus more on their fear or aversion to others, than listening to commands when they are in social environments, which means that at times they will completely ignore their training.

Benefits of A Personalized Training Approach

I used the example of the different types of kids in school because I want you to think back to your school days. Not one person could learn in the exact same way that another person could learn.

Some students use flashcards, some reread the entire handbook a million times over, some need to see their work being applied practically, and some can just listen to the teacher and get it without an issue. Each student has their own style of learning, and just like that so does each puppy.

If you were to take a blanket approach to how puppies are trained, you might find yourself completely failing in teaching some puppies. For example, the laidback puppy will need a quiet area where they can train alone and might only be able to accept encouragement in the form of a single pet, or a treat. Whereas the sweet-natured puppy will respond even in a large crowd and respond better to more excitement and affection.

A personalized approach helps you to ensure that your training goes as easily and fast as possible. At the same time, you will continue to build on the relationship between you and your puppy positively and strengthen the bond the two of you share.

Tips and Techniques for Observing And Identifying Your Puppy's Personality Traits

By now you should have a basic idea of the type of personality that your puppy might have. I do, however, want to take this opportunity to remind you that just like humans each puppy is

extremely unique. So, while the chances are good that they might fit into one of the types I outlined for you above, they might not be exactly as I explained the type. This is why it is extremely important that you identify your companion's personality traits for yourself.

Keeping A Puppy Journal

One of the best ways to identify your pup's personality traits is to keep a puppy journal. This is not the only benefit of a puppy journal, however. The best way I can share the benefits of a puppy journal is to share a story with you. I know of a couple who have the most beautiful golden retrievers. Both of these retrievers fit quite well into the laidback personality type. They are eager to please, love everyone, and get very excited. The problem, however, is that they both suffer from anxiety. Their owners have gone so far as to install cameras all around their property and get hourly updates regarding the weather at their homes. You see, if there is a slight rumble from thunder, the dogs get so anxious that they have in the past taken windows and doors out with their sheer fear. This makes it difficult for their owners to go on holiday, visit friends, or even go into the office.

To make life a bit easier for everyone, they started a puppy journal. This journal includes what their dogs fear, how the dogs react, what the dogs do when they start to get anxious (they will hold your hand in their mouth, and the pressure with which they hold your hand indicates their anxiety levels, or they will go fetch their own anxiety blankets and lay against you biting down on these blankets.) This journal also includes information on where

their medicine is, the family vet, cute little tips and tricks to help them calm down, what they are allowed to eat, what they are not allowed to eat, and what to do when they need to leave the house to ensure the dogs are as safe as possible.

This puppy journal has become their ultimate guide for pet sitters or friends who help out when the owners can't get home themselves.

That is the idea behind a puppy journal. It will help you to track everything from personality traits to training techniques and progress, allergies, medical history including vaccination records, care instructions, and even memories of their time with you.

There is another benefit to the puppy journal as well. When you use it to track things like your puppy's eating habits, weight, bowel movements, behavioral changes, injuries, and other pertinent information, you will be the most well-prepared client that your vet has. They will appreciate this. Remember, when you go to a doctor, you can tell the doctor what is wrong with you, where it hurts, how you feel, etc. A vet needs to experiment, guess, and observe to get simple answers from their patients. Having all this extra information that you can record in your puppy journal will give the vet a better idea of where to start with their investigation which could not only save them valuable time but might even help your wallet by eliminating the need for extensive tests and repeat consultations to discover the cause of any issues your dog might be having.

Behavioral Patterns and Stimuli Responses

The best way to determine a puppy's personality is to see it in action. This means that you will need to see their normal behavior when they are left to do as they please and see how they respond to different stimulants.

When you are looking at their behavioral patterns you will want to observe them in an environment where there are little to no stimulants. Think of this as during the day when you are busy working, what does your puppy do? This can be difficult to gauge if you do not work from home. Rest assured, there will be signs. Look to see whether their toys have been moved around, ask your neighbors if they heard barking, or saw your puppy doing anything outside, and look to see if any of your belongings have been chewed or moved around. These will all give you an idea of what your puppy did when you were not there. Of course, you can also invest in a camera that can be placed in the house to check on the puppy.

While this will help you to get an idea of their behavioral patterns on their own, it is still not a direct observation and just a guessing game. So, when you are home you need to pay extra attention to your puppy and record what you see in their puppy journal. Look specifically at things like where your puppy is when you are not busy playing or training. Are they lying on top, or next to you? Or are they lying in their crate or outside? Or, are they busy playing with a toy or maybe another animal? Does your dog tend to bring their toys closer to you, or do they run off and go play in another room? These are merely examples of the

behavior that your dog will show which can give you an idea of their personalities.

Once you have established their basic behavior patterns, you can start looking at their responses to stimulants. This will be how they react to changes in their environment. When it is feeding time, do they run towards their food, or do they wait patiently for you to fill their bowl? Do they eat everything in one sitting, or do they take their time? The same goes for when you get home from work or when a visitor arrives. Even looking at how they interact with other pets around them will give you valuable insight.

Any type of stimulant will give you an idea of how your new pet will react and what their personality is. So be creative and expose them to any stimulant you can think of. Record every action and reaction they have, and sit down and analyze what these responses of them mean.

Accuracy Through Patience and Consistency

To ensure that you find the correct personality type for your new companion, you will need to be accurate. As we've seen when we look at the different personality types that your pet might have, it is easy to confuse certain personality types with each other. The reason for this is that there are certain traits that are shared by more than one archetype. For example, both sweet-natured and adaptable puppies tend to want to please their humans. So, when you notice this behavior you might find it difficult to distinguish which one of these two personality archetypes best fits your

pup's personality. The key to discovering this is to be accurate in your observations through being both patient and consistent.

Of course, this also relates to your training methods. In a moment we'll look into how you can use your knowledge of your pup's personality to ensure that your training method is tailored to the exact needs of your puppy. When you start to use this training method on your puppy you need to ensure that you remain consistent in your approach. When you start to make changes to your training techniques after you have already started to teach your puppy, it can and will lead to them becoming confused.

Additionally, your assessment of your pup's personality might not be as accurate as you might think. Let me explain; when you throw the ball to your puppy, they might be quite good at picking it up and bringing it back to you. This might make you think that they are a people pleaser and could be quite easy to train. Until you try and teach them something else, and you start to realize that, in fact, they are better at playing around than taking commands. When they brought you their ball, it's not because they were learning correct behavior, but instead that the game just suited their wants at that moment.

Patience and consistency do not end there. You need to have constant patience with your puppy during their training and learning. In fact, you need to have patience even after that as your puppy will more than likely make mistakes during their lifetime. This means that you will need to learn how to be patient at any time during the course of your time with your puppy.

How To Use Your Knowledge to Tailor Your Training Approach

As we've already established, your pup's personality will determine how you approach their training. You will need to look into what training technique works best for your pup and how you can adjust your training techniques as your dog's needs change and their personality grows.

Choosing the Most Effective Training Technique

When it comes to the training of your puppy, you need to take more than just their personality into account. You need to look at their temperament as well. It's important that you understand that there is a difference between personality and temperament. Your puppy might have a laid-back personality but be what we call a "front of the line" temperament. This might seem contradictory in some cases, but let's look at the three main temperament archetypes to help you better understand what I mean.

A front-of-the-line dog tends to be the leader of the pack. These are the dogs that know themselves quite well. They know what they like, and what they don't like. They also know what they want to do, and what they do not want to do. These are the dogs that will need a strong personality to train them. You need to be able to take control of the situation and be firm and direct with them, otherwise, they might not listen to you at all. A common misconception is that these pups tend to be from larger breeds such as Rottweilers or any of the Shepherd family. In truth, even a little Dachshund can have a front-of-the-line temperament. When these pets are assured that they have a strong leader in

their life, they will be more inclined to show you their true personality which might otherwise be hidden beneath a harsh temperament.

A middle-of-the-line dog might share similarities with front-of-the-line dogs. This means that they require a similar approach in regard to strictness. However, these dogs tend to take direction a lot easier and are usually the easiest to train. While a front-of-the-line dog tends to have a more dominating temperament that could often make way for aggression in the form of over-protectiveness, your middle-of-the-line puppy will tend to lean towards one of the more playful personalities. When these pups feel that they do not have strong leadership, they might end up acting out in more energetic and playful ways. These are the type of dogs that will most probably ignore you and continue laying in their bed when you try and get them to go for a walk when they don't want to, or they will completely ignore you when they are playing.

The other temperament archetype we will be looking at is the back-of-the-line dogs. They are so-called because they are the ones who prefer to hang back and let someone else take the lead. While this might sound like they are easier to train, it in fact does make it harder to train them. These pups are usually more cautious, which makes it harder to get them to learn something new. At the same time, they are also more sensitive, so if you become impatient even once, or you act too strict with them they might end up becoming fearful and stressed out instead of taking in what they are supposed to be learning.

Each temperament requires its own approach just as each personality requires its own approach. When you combine the two you will be able to identify the best technique to be used to train your pet. For example, a front-of-the-line and sweet-natured puppy will require you to be strict with them and take on a leadership role but be more easily taught through showing your approval to them.

Think of their personality as showing you what tools to use, and which tools to avoid. At the same time, their temperament shows you whether you should be a drill sergeant or a kindergarten teacher.

Examples of Different Personality Requirements

I would love to take a moment to look into the different personality types and give you a working example of how to approach each personality in their training.

Let's start with our confident personality archetypes. Since these pups tend to not fear anything, they usually have a front-of-the-line temperament. This means that you will need to be strict in your approach to their training. Ideally, you would start off with their training in a private setting where they will not be distracted by other pets. However, make sure that during this time they are still socialized quite often so they do not become anti-social. Once they have some of the basic training, you can start introducing stimuli like other pets or people. Start with just one other pet, and once their training is upheld around this pet, add another. Eventually, you will have full control of your confident pup even when you are in a crowd. When you have a free-

spirited pup, they tend to display middle or back-of-the-line temperaments. It's extremely important to identify the correct temperament in these pups before you start doing their training. For a middle free-spirited pup your training would also be quite strict, but instead of keeping them away from other pups to encourage them to listen to you, you will need to direct them towards other animals to help them to be more comfortable in the presence of others. While with back-of-the-line free-spirited pups, you will need to gently ease them through these social interactions while upholding their training instead of being strict with them.

The laidback puppy will most often have a middle-of-the-line temperament. This would mean that they are extremely prone to outbursts of energy when they become excited. While you might need to be extremely strict with their training, it could mean that it will take longer to introduce them to their training in a social environment than it would take a front-of-the-line confident puppy. However, once you do introduce them to a social environment while training, you probably would not need to be as strict as with the confident example.

Up next, we have our adaptable puppies. These pups tend to have either front or middle-of-the-line temperaments. However, their great adaptability makes it a lot easier to train them than other puppies. This means that you need not worry too much about finding a private place for them. You can use their walks and visits to the park for their training, just remember to still give them a lot of free time at both of these events, so they do not see the park or their walk as a chore, but also as a chance to enjoy themselves. You also tend to be less strict with these pups

than you would be with other pups that share their temperament.

Lastly, the sweet-natured pup. The pups tend to have back-of-the-line temperaments. They will often shy away from other dogs, but they are not too bothered by their existence in the vicinity. So, you may be able to train your sweet-natured pup with other dogs around. Their attention by nature will more than likely already be on you, and you should be able to bring out your full kindergarten teacher approach on them since they respond better to affection and positive reinforcement.

Adjusting Training Methods

So far, I've tried to reinforce the idea that you need to remain consistent in your training method. But what happens when your furry friend stops responding to the training techniques you've been using so far?

The short answer is to adjust your training method immediately. However, that can lead to confusion and a setback when done incorrectly. The best advice I can give you is to stop the training immediately and reassess the reasons you had for using the technique you are currently using. Then look at what went wrong with your current training technique. Were you too strict or not strict enough? Were there too many stimulants or was there some other factor that caused the training to fail?

The most important task for you is to identify where it went wrong and work on changing that, instead of changing the entire routine. Let's say for example your puppy used to completely

ignore other pets when you started training him or her. Now after a while of training, they have become more comfortable and more social around other pets. This is a good thing since this is most probably what you have been aiming to achieve. The downside, however, is that they might now end up being more interested in their new friends, than in what you are trying to teach them.

In this example, it is quite easy to identify why the training is no longer working, and why you elected to train them around other pets. While the obvious choice is to stop training them around other pets, this can be counterproductive. They might start thinking that they are doing something wrong by interacting with other pets and stop doing that again. Or they might think that the other pets are doing something wrong and start getting aggressive towards them.

The better idea in adjusting these training methods is to reduce the amount of pets around your puppy while training them, and then slowly increase the number of pets again until your puppy follows their training while in a crowd.

Adjusting your training does not mean changing it completely, instead, it means making small changes that will keep your pet comfortable but align your training to fit better into their new needs. I also want you to remember that when you need to adjust your training techniques it does not mean that you are doing something wrong. In actual fact, dogs are better at changing their personalities than humans are. You just need to be able to keep up with them.

Puppy Personality Quiz

Figuring out your canine companion's personality on your own can be extremely difficult. So, I've developed a personality quiz for you to use. This quiz will give you a pretty good idea of what personality your puppy has. While I made it with the idea of being as accurate as possible, it should still only be used to guide you in the right direction and not be a definitive answer. Try as I might, it's very difficult to be the puppy whisperer when you only meet the puppy by being ink on a page.

Question 1

Your neighbor just found out you have a new puppy and invites you to their weekly furry fun day where all the neighborhood pets and their humans get together. When you walk in what is your puppy's reaction?

A: Runs in to meet the other friends, and completely forgets that you exist among the fun they are having.

B: Walks in and bullies the other pets immediately.

C: Seems completely indifferent at times and goes completely bonkers at other times.

D: Walks in and greets everyone as if they have known each other since birth. Also somehow manages to act more appropriately than other dogs who have been there for a long time.

E: Suddenly becomes glued to your side and doesn't want to go near any of the other furry friends.

Question 2

The word of the day is independence, and your puppy is...

A: So Independent the day you got them they picked you up, not the other way around. In the car, they told you about their 401K. It's better than yours.

B: Independence is their middle name, they don't need you for anything. Yet they are clueless when it comes to interacting with others.

C: They're pretty independent, but somehow tend to end up in someone's personal space all the time.

D: Yes, they can be independent at times, but when the urge gets them, and they want that human interaction, they can be extremely needy.

E: They are currently on your lap where they've been since the moment you met.

Question 3

You just bought your puppy a new toy, what is their reaction?

A: This toy, just like all the other toys belongs to them now. If they're playing with it and anyone else tries to get close, they can expect a snap.

B: It better be a toy they like. And don't even think about forcing them to play with it if they don't like it.

C: TOY! Nothing else exists. If anything is in their way it gets run over. This includes people, objects, and other pets. Your pup doesn't even see them.

D: Oh, you bought them a toy? Put it over there with the rest in its place where it will be played with at the appropriate times.

E: It's not as good as you. They might play with it when you try and engage them with it, but that's about it.

Question 4

You just tried to teach your puppy how to sit. How did it go?

A: Quite good. Your pup learned it. But they still like to decide for themselves when they want to sit and where.

B: Somehow you ended up being the one sitting on command.

C: The moment they sat down they got so happy they did it, that they forgot they were supposed to be sitting.

D: They were born to do this. It took them no time to figure out what you want and even less time to perfect their sit on their own.

E: You could hear them asking "Is this right? Is this how I should be doing it? Are you pleased with me? How can I do it better?"

Question 5

Your family came over, it took about five seconds for your cousin's kids to start fighting. Where is your pup?

A: They already pushed the kids down and took complete control of the situation.

B: Sitting to the side, daring those kids to get too close or someone to try and push them towards those kids.

C: They see the fights as playtime and are jumping in between having a massive ball!

D: They are barely aware of the fight and completely unphased when they do become aware of it.

E: In your arms shivering like a naked camel at the North Pole.

The Results

Now that you have chosen the answers that best suit your puppy, it's time to figure out what they mean. Each answer has a point connected to it. The following is what each answer is the point for each answer.

All "A" answers get four points.
All "B" answers get three points.
All "C" answers get two points.
All "D" answers get one point.
All "E" answers get five points.

Once you've tallied up the total points that your pets have gotten on the quiz, you can use the below formula to determine which personality archetype they are most likely to fall under.

5–9 points mean they are an adaptable puppy.
10–14 points mean they are laidback.
15–19 points mean they are free-spirited.
20–24 points mean they are confident.
25 points mean they are sweet-natured.

Remember, this is an estimation and should not be seen as a rule written in stone. It is possible for some pups to fall into a certain personality type but still display traits from other personality

types especially when you take their temperament into consideration.

TWO

Home Harmony

W hen new mothers bring their baby home from the hospital for the first time, they have done every other piece of preparation they can think of. You don't need to go through the same amount of trouble, but there is still a lot of preparation to do. You also need to introduce your puppy to your family and their new space, and then figure out how to adapt the existing dynamic to this new addition.

Preparing Your Home for The New Puppy's Arrival

The first step is to prepare your home. You need to know what items you need in your home, what needs to be removed, and how the environment should be changed to suit your new arrival.

The New Arrival Checklist

Figuring out what items you need for your new four-legged family member can be difficult. Luckily this list remains fairly constant for every new puppy. Here is a general easy-to-follow checklist of everything you need to have ready before your puppy joins the family.

- **a Crate:** This will be the safe place for your puppy. While I understand that there are concerns about crates for some pet lovers, we will address those concerns later on in the book. You might also believe that a crate is not necessary because your pup will sleep on the bed with you. I'm still going to encourage you to get a crate for them so that they can have a safe space to retreat to if they ever feel like they need to.
- **puppy Bed:** Once again, whether your pup will enjoy your furniture or not, giving them their own bed is essential to helping them have their own space in which they can feel comfortable.
- **playpen:** A brand-new puppy will not be house-trained. They will go to the toilet in your home, they will bite everything they see, and they will hurt themselves. A playpen will help you to restrict their movements temporarily until they are better trained. This will not only protect your home, but it will also keep your new addition safe.
- **food:** This goes without explanation. Your puppy needs to eat. But we need to put this on the list for two reasons. The first is that often in our excitement, we forget the

most basic of things. When you choose your pet's food you also need to look into getting healthy and appropriate food. My personal suggestion is to speak to your vet. They will be able to point you to the best food available in your area.

- **treats:** Treats will not only be used for training, but also for bribing! When your puppy comes home the chances are that they will be fairly scared of the new environment, away from their siblings and the only humans they have known so far. To help them learn that they are in a safe and friendly space, and to help them to start trusting and loving you, you can bribe them with treats.

- **name tags:** I know every time I decided to get a new puppy, I picked out a name before I even thought the decision through. This is a good thing. It means you can be prepared. Get a name tag for your puppy with their name, your telephone number, and home address on it. That way if your puppy turns out to be a little Houdini in the making then you know they'll find their way back to you.

- **food & water bowls:** This is another one of those items that are so obvious that you can easily forget them. My first puppy got treated to my good dining set because I forgot to buy them their own bowls. I would suggest getting stainless steel bowls. They are easier to clean and less likely to contain harmful plastics.

- **play toys:** Puppies require a lot of attention and stimulation. This might not always be possible in the hustle of modern life. So, make sure that you have toys

galore. Try everything from chew toys to dental chews, and even your normal soft toys and balls. When your puppy is still young and teething, you might want to look into focusing more on chew toys and reserve soft toys for times when you can ensure they don't completely destroy them and create choking hazards for themselves.

- **comfort toys:** Yes, there is a difference. While play toys are meant to stimulate your puppy, comfort toys are meant to calm them down in your absence. These comfort toys are usually equipped with electronics that help to mimic the heartbeat and warmth of their littermates that may no longer be there with them. It can be an invaluable tool to help them adjust to their new environment and get them more comfortable at sleep time.

- **toy box:** Unless you are planning on falling all over puppy toys each day, a toy box is a must. Research the average height of your pup's breed and decide whether you want them to have access to their own toy box or not. Then get a box that will suit your needs. Even if your pup is able to remove their own toys at a later stage, they will be trained by then and more than likely cause less destruction. This will not only keep your home clean from toys and toy parts but also help to keep the toys intact for longer.

- **emergency plan:** New life is fragile. Add that to Murphy's law and the fact that no matter how well you prepare, there is always the possibility of something going wrong, and you'll understand the need for an emergency plan. Before you even get your puppy, start

asking people in your area which vet they recommend, and why. Then call or visit each vet office in your area and see if you agree with your friend's assessments. You don't need to speak to a vet directly, but you can speak to their reception staff to gather some information. Do they offer emergency services? What are their prices for basic check-ups, vaccinations, and emergency consultations? Do they accept any type of animal insurance? Get as much information as you can to ensure that if something does go wrong with your new puppy, you are fully prepared and know where you can go and who you can call. I also suggest that you schedule a "new pet exam" with your chosen veterinary clinic/hospital in the first week you have your new puppy. There is no comparison to the peace of mind of having a professional telling you that your new pup is completely healthy. And if they are not, you got ahead of whatever ailment they may have.

- **training plan:** Your training starts the moment that the puppy is in your presence. They will be young and vulnerable. They will take social and behavioral cues from you. So be sure that you already have a plan of action for their training so that you can hit the ground running and ensure that you achieve success as soon as possible.
- **collars:** Those name tags we got need to go somewhere. Keep in mind your pup's fur has an impact on which collar you should use. Long-haired breeds prefer light and material collars that are less likely to pull on their hair, while short-haired breeds prefer using silicone collars. You should be able to fit two fingers into the

collar snugly while your new puppy is wearing it. Remember as your puppy grows, the collar will become tighter.

- **harnesses:** A collar is great, but a harness is better. The reason for this is that collars only attach around the neck of your pup. This can cause problems later on with both their necks and spines being injured. A harness offers better support by wrapping around the body of your pup, which means less chance of injury, as well as more control over your pup. Harnesses are also more difficult to escape than collars. This is why harnesses are quickly becoming the preferred tool for walking, especially if your dog is a strong puller. Front, or chest lead harnesses (where the leash attaches at the front of the chest instead of between the shoulder blades on their back) are a miracle worker for strong pulling dogs.
- **leashes:** Your leash also needs quite a bit of thinking and planning. How long do you want your leash to be? What material will work best for you? If you have a puppy who tends to get excited you might want to get a leash that is softer on your hands, but if your puppy is from a breed that will grow bigger and stronger than others, you will need to make sure it's strong and durable.
- **brush:** While short-haired breeds don't need that much brushing, a brush is still needed to help your puppy get rid of any dirt or foreign objects that may get stuck in their coat. Plus, being brushed can be such a calming experience for your puppy that it may help you win over their trust.

- **poop-scoop/waste bag:** Whether your puppy will be running around in your yard, or in a park, a poop-scoop or a doggy waste bag is an essential item for any dog owner. It makes cleaning up after them much quicker and easier. Plus, it is against the law to not pick up after your pet in most public places.
- **toothbrush:** Yes, I am very serious. Dogs also have dental hygiene that need to be cared for. Ask your vet for advice on brushing and ensure that your pup never has bad breath or loses their teeth way too early. They can also suffer from tooth pain and infection, and that is something I don't even wish upon my arch-nemesis!
- **toothpaste:** No, they can't just use yours. Pups get their own toothpaste! Ask your vet or check your local pet store for the brush and the toothpaste
- **shampoo:** Just like with their dental health, your puppy has normal hygiene that also needs to be cared for. While your puppy does not need to take a bath as often as we humans do, they still need to be cleaned. Doggy shampoo helps to ensure that any dirt and odors get removed from their fur. There are also special shampoos to help prevent ticks and fleas from turning your companion's coat into their new home. As someone who has had tick-bite fever themselves, this is not something you want your puppy to go through. Please consult your vet on the proper shampoo for your specific pet.
- **puppy journal:** As I've mentioned before, this is your puppy diary. Everything anyone ever needs to know about them will be on these pages. Having it ready when

they first get home means you can start filling the pages immediately.

This checklist should complete your puppy preparations. If you get everything that is on this list, you should have absolutely no issues when your pup comes home for the first time. They will have everything their heart desires, and you will have created a welcoming space for them.

Time to Puppy-Proof

So now that you brought everything into the home that your puppy will need, you need to look into what needs to be removed or hidden from them to ensure their safety. Just like how you would put locks on cabinets and soft edges on the corners of everything when you bring a baby home, you need to adjust your home a bit to make it better suited for a four-legged terror ball of love.

- **electrical cords:** No, I will not show you my laptop charging cable. Yes, it might have two or three places where it's been repaired. Puppies love chewing! Electrical cables can be so tempting, and equally as dangerous. While it may not be possible to completely get rid of these cords, you can unplug any that might not be necessary and use cord concealers to hide the rest together.
- **human food:** Yes, we are all guilty of it at some stage. When those big puppy dog eyes meet yours, and that cute tiny paw makes its way toward your food, and the teeny

tiny little tail starts wagging, it's hard to say no. Unfortunately, human food is heavily processed and spiced, and puppy stomachs just are not made to handle this. This habit will also teach your puppy to beg and try and take food from your plates. A trait that you do not want to teach. Feeding certain foods can also have dire health consequences. Chocolate is the most well-known human food NOT to feed dogs. There are many more toxic foods such as avocados, grapes, cooked bones, onions, garlic, and alcohol, to name a few.

- **medication:** Just like a young child, your puppy won't understand that medication is dangerous and should be avoided. If they can reach it, the chances are they will try and eat it. So, make sure your medication is all packed away in cupboards too high for your craft little companion to reach. Believe me when I say, I've seen puppies get into places I struggle to get into!

- **toilets:** You most probably saw a few cartoons that showed dogs drinking water out of the toilet. Aside from the fact this is disgusting, your toilet will either have lots of bacteria in it or lots of chemicals to kill those bacteria. Neither of these are safe for canine consumption. Then there is also the possibility that your puppy could fall into the toilet and drown. So, it's best to keep the toilet lid closed at all times. So, women, if the men in your house keep forgetting to put the seat down, this is your lucky day!

- **doors and windows:** While your puppy is still young and new to the world, they can be their own biggest hazard. An open door or window beckons them to explore the

outside world where they have not yet learned the dangers of other animals, metal monstrosities, or the dangers of losing their way and forgetting where home is.

- **blinds and curtains:** Look at your blinds or curtains, most of them will have some sort of string or cable connected to them. Whether it is to tie them down or to control whether they open or close. These strings and cables can be a hazard for your puppy, as they will most likely try to bite on them and in their playfulness can get entangled and hurt themselves. Make sure you can secure these higher than your puppy can jump.

- **small items:** Take a moment and look at the environment around you. Count the number of objects around you that you can fit through your watch or bracelet. These are all choking hazards for your new pup. They should all be moved somewhere safe where your pup cannot reach them, like into a drawer.

- **sharp objects:** This goes without saying, and I'm pretty confident you've already looked at this. But just for the sake of safety, I have included it in our list. Any razors, knives, scissors, tweezers, nail clippers, screwdrivers, or anything else that might have a sharp point to it should also be packed away. Your puppy does not understand danger yet and can easily hurt themselves by thinking these sharp objects are toys.

- **trashcans:** While your puppy is still learning their environment there are some basic things that they don't need to learn, like how to use their nose to find food. We all discard items that might draw their attention into our

trashcans, and even if we don't the explorative nature of a puppy can cause them to end up in the trash can in any case. Make sure your trash can is in a place where your puppy cannot get to it, or it is secured so your pup can't open it or even push it over.

- **plants:** Both inside and outside of the house you might have poisonous or toxic plants. Take some time and research what effects the plants you have can have on canine companions. Either remove or simply move the dangerous plants to someplace where your tiny terror cannot get to them while they learn that not everything should go into their mouth.

- **yard fences:** If it is possible and your yard has not yet been fenced off, I would strongly suggest doing so. Not only does it add an extra layer of security to ensure your pup doesn't escape into the streets, but it also effectively enlarges the area your puppy has to be safe and comfortable in.

- **pools:** While swimming is a natural instinct, that does not mean your puppy will be any good at it. Many dogs never gain the ability to swim and end up sinking like a rock when they meet a body of water. If you have a pool, even an above-ground pool (some crafty pups learn how to climb ladders before they learn how to chew their food) make sure that you fence that off as well.

- **fertilizer, pesticide, insecticide:** When you treat your lawn or garden with any of these you should keep your pup away from it for a while. At least until it has settled in and dissipated a bit. Pesticides and insecticides both

have chemicals in them that can be harmful to your pup's health, and fertilizer will make them dirty and smelly.

- **purses and bags:** Whether it is just a school backpack, a laptop bag, or a purse filled with every life-essential item known to women, these collections of fuzzy ends and strings are extremely tempting for your puppy. But they won't stay contained to the extra bits, before you know it your puppy will make their way into the bag, and might destroy what is inside. Plastic book covers, perfume bottles, toxic medications, credit cards, pens, and anything that you carry in these bags becomes fair game.

- **cleaning supplies:** Most of us keep our cleaning chemicals in the cupboard under the sink. It's just one of those traditions that have become unwritten laws. Please make sure that this cupboard does not only close properly, but that you can lock it as well before your curious pup finds his way in there and makes a meal of these chemicals.

- **heights:** While your puppy is still learning what hurts, and what is dangerous, they might be fearless little adrenaline chasers, or at least it will seem like this. Until they understand that falling from a great height, like three stairs up, can lead to broken bones and excruciating pain, you need to help look after them and keep them away from heights where they could easily fall off. This includes being on the couch without supervision and even in the arms of small children who are still clumsy themselves.

- **heat sources:** While most homes have some sort of
  central heating that is pushed through air vents, there are
  still some that have radiators, gas heaters, and fireplaces.
  Aside from these your hair dryer, hair straightener, oven,
  or even backyard grill are all sources of heat that can
  pose a danger to your pup. Cover up or block off these
  areas so your puppy cannot get close enough to these
  heat sources to get hurt.

These are the main issues to be on the lookout for. If you can restrict access to the elements I mentioned above, or better yet, remove these dangers from your home completely, you should have a home that is nearly completely puppy-safe and ready to welcome your newest family member.

Puppy Spaces

You know how sometimes you just want to get in bed and not get up again? When you feel like you just don't have the energy for the world that day? Your dog has similar feelings and emotions. Sometimes they just feel like they've had enough social time and need to take a break. This is where their own space comes in.

These puppy-safe spaces are not just for them, however. I would like to start by looking at the possible benefits of giving your pup their own space.

- It's a lot safer. When you have designated areas for your
  puppy to be in, especially areas that are blocked off to
  keep them in, you have a smaller area to worry about

puppy-proofing and you are more assured that they won't end up in the road, the pool, or falling off somewhere they are not supposed to be at.

- It's comfortable for them. You can add special toys and furniture in these areas that your pup can enjoy without any type of restriction. When you really allow them to make these areas their own, they will eventually find themselves being completely at ease in these areas which will grant them a safe space when there are stressors or unwanted stimuli like your visiting nieces and nephews who don't know how to play nice.

- It allows trouble-free playtime. When they are in their space away from stress or dangers, they are not the only ones who will enjoy the lack of stress. You can be assured that no matter what they play with or what they get up to, they won't get into any sort of trouble.

- It's terrific for training. Did you know that dogs also live by the rule of "don't poop where you eat." For them, this rule is a bit more literal. Dogs don't like it when places they frequent are dirty and smelly. This means when you create a space for them, they will more than likely try to go potty outside of that area, which can make their house training go a lot easier.

- It's completely cleanable. When they have a comfortable space that they can enjoy themselves in, they will choose to do so more often than being in other areas. This means that their toys, shed fur, and even accidents are more likely to be confined to these areas, even if they have free reign of the home. This can make your task of cleaning up after them much simpler.

- It might act as a teaching aid. You can use this puppy space as a tool to teach your children about respecting boundaries and personal space. Allowing your children to learn that when the puppy goes into a certain area of the home, or into their playpen or kennel, all on their own, means the puppy is tired and wants to rest now. Not only will this help to show your young ones how to communicate their own needs, and respect the needs of those around them, but it will also reduce the chances of your kid or puppy getting hurt. Remember, puppies will most likely see your kids as just larger bipedal littermates. And siblings tend to fight all the time.

There are several other ways to create a space for your puppy both inside and outside of the home. One of the most popular, effective, and easy ways to do both is to make use of a puppy playpen.

These can easily be constructed, deconstructed, and changed to suit your pup's needs. You can also easily move the playpen from inside to outside, and back inside again. You should always use the same area for your pet so that when they outgrow their pen, they still know which areas are specifically for them.

At this time, you can easily just put up a gate at the entrances to these areas that can be closed when your pup needs to stay in their area, or left open when they should have free reign of the home.

There are some important points to remember regarding your puppy spaces;

- Keep the area comfortable. Pups need areas slightly cooler than we do, and they need their own furniture to lay on and relax so that they are off the hard floors.
- Do not use this space to encourage play or work. This is where your pup needs to relax and do what they prefer.
- Your pup should have as much choice as possible about when they are in their safe space or not.
- This is not a time-out or training zone.
- Your pup should not be completely isolated in these zones. It is important they still have social interactions when they need it.

Of course, getting them to start using this area as a safe space can be difficult in the beginning. Luckily there are some tricks you can use to help them get used to relaxing here. Aside from their normal feeding in there, whenever you see them enter this area out of their own free will you can give them a treat. In this way, they will start to associate this area with a positive reward. You can get them a long-lasting treat, or an interactive feeder that will release food or treats over some time while they are playing with it. The longer they spend in this space alone and get rewarded for doing so, the more they will learn that this is the space where being alone is a good thing.

How To Introduce the Puppy to Its New Environment and Family Members

So, you are as well prepared as you can be, you are prepared for your pup's arrival, you know what to expect, and your home has been set up. Now you need to actually bring your puppy home. This in itself is a major event. You cannot just bring the puppy home and leave them to discover the world on their own. All the new faces, the new environment, the loneliness, it will just be too much to handle. Plus, this poor creature won't know how to act, or react in this new environment.

Step-By-Step Instructions on Introducing Your Puppy to Its New Home and Family

I've compiled a step-by-step instruction guide to help you know exactly what to do when you introduce your puppy to your home and their new family.

1. Let them learn your scent. If possible, do this before they even come home. If the breeder or rescue you are getting your puppy from allows it, then an old piece of clothing with your scent on it will go a long way to helping them become comfortable with you.
2. Bring them into their home alone for the first time but stay close. This will let them explore the area at their own pace while using you as a safety blanket.
3. Once they have become a bit more comfortable with their environment you can start letting family members in one-by-one. Let them remain calm and let the puppy

approach them. Don't rush it, and don't bribe the puppy with food.

4. If at any time your puppy becomes overwhelmed by this whole process, do not chase everyone away. Instead, gently remove the puppy from the room, take them to another room, and let them calm down and relax. Then slowly reintroduce them to the original room.

5. Once your puppy has met all the other human family members and become completely comfortable with them, you can start to bring in the other animals. This should occur on neutral ground. So perhaps move to a neighbor's yard, or have the introduction take place at the park. It is also a good idea to make sure both dogs are well-fed and played out before meeting each other so that any excess energy or "hangry" emotions are worked out before the meeting.

6. We'll start with other dogs. Before introducing the dogs to each other, introduce the scents to each other. You can use the pre-existing dog's toys or even their bed to give the new puppy the scent, and the shirt or jersey that you've been wearing is perfect for your pre-existing dog since it will mix both your scent and that of the new puppy.

7. Once both dogs have had each other's scent, you can with the help of a family member introduce the two to each other. Make sure you have control over both dogs so you can move them away at a moment's notice. Remember not to rush them either, let them calmly start to move towards each other at their own pace. If your pre-existing buddy gets a bit too excited and it seems like the

puppy becomes uncomfortable or vice versa, calmly create some space between them and calm both of them down before you let them near each other again.

8. Once they have each other's scent rinse and repeat this process with all the other dogs you may have. Make sure you start this process with the calmest dog, and give your puppy more than enough time between meeting new dogs to adjust to this extra identity. We do not want to overwhelm them.

9. Next, we'll introduce your puppy to cats. They are somewhat different than dogs and these meetings can occur inside of the home. Once again make sure both animals are fed and have gotten rid of excess energy before you start.

10. The first introduction between canine and feline should take place in a very controlled environment as the animosity between these two species is not always just cartoon antics. The best idea is to either have each of them in their own separate crates and push these next to each other or to have them separated by a playpen gate. Let them have the security of some sort of object between them, while also having enough freedom and space to get to each other and interact.

11. When the animals respond positively towards each other, praise them and reward this behavior. When they respond negatively, create some space and calm them down. Be careful when you calm them down to do it in a way that they do not feel like they are being rewarded.

12. Allocate a safe space for your cat where the puppy cannot go, a safe space for your puppy where the cat cannot go,

and a neutral ground where they can get to know each other on their own terms.

13. Lastly, during the initial few days of the puppy being home, be careful to not neglect your children, or other pets in favor of the puppy. While it is exciting, and you most probably feel overprotective over the puppy (young animals are actually cute by design. This is nature's way of making sure they survive) if you give the puppy too much attention and the others too little, they might feel abandoned and start to resent your new puppy.

And there you go. 13 Easy steps to ensure that your puppy meets their new family in a positive and happy environment that will help to create a familial bond between this newest addition, and your already present loved ones.

Tips to Help Your New Puppy Adjust

Regardless of how well you prepared your home and your family for the newest addition, there will always be a period after your puppy has joined the household that they will still need to adjust to their new environment, family dynamics, and family schedule. There are some ways in which you can help to make this adjustment easier for your furry friend.

- Start enforcing rules from the beginning. This might sound like it's too early, but the faster they learn what is allowed and what is not, the faster they will adjust to their new environment,
- Keep a close eye on their initial explorations. Your puppy is the best indicator of how the environment needs to be changed to help them adapt. Keep an eye on what makes them uncomfortable, or what leads them to mischief so that you can change the environment, or their behavior as needed.
- Make sure they have something appropriate to chew on. While they are teething, they will chew on anything that they can find. When they start chewing on something they are not supposed to, like your favorite pair of shoes, redirect their attention to their chew toy.
- Start following their routine immediately. If you plan on taking them for a walk every day after work, do so from day one, even if this walk is just to the front yard.
- Have their potty and sleeping spots sorted before they come home, and make sure to both show them where these are and encourage them to use them from the start. When they do use these spots appropriately you should reward and encourage them to continue doing so.
- Be patient. They will not get everything right the first time around, and that is okay. Give them time to learn and adapt, and eventually, you will see the results you are hoping for.

Strategies for Creating a Harmonious Household With Your New Furry Family Member

In the previous section, I mentioned some tips for helping your puppy to adapt to your household. This is an extremely important aspect of creating a harmonious household. If the puppy cannot fit in with your family, it will cause you a lot more than just a few headaches. So to help you ensure your puppy fits in perfectly, I want to focus on establishing both routines and boundaries, as well as why consistency during their training is important.

- Establish rules and boundaries. This helps to teach pups where their boundaries are.
- Teach your puppy that trusting you not only comes with rewards but that it brings a positive outcome into their lives.
- Don't treat your puppy like a baby who needs to be picked up and carried everywhere or consoled after every hiccup. This can lead to inadvertently encouraging negative behavior.

The Second Pup

If this is your second pup being brought home, you should be extremely careful to ensure that they respect the boundaries of your other dog as well. Remember that you and your human family are not the only ones with personalities, your other dog will also have their own unique outlook on life, and their own likes, dislikes, and pet peeves.

For at least the first few months there are some precautions you will need to take:

- Feed the dogs in separate spaces. This will teach them that they each have their own bowl of food and that there is no danger of their food being stolen or needing to be shared.
- Control what they play with and what they chew on when they are together. If you see any toys or chews that are contentious or that cause any type of problem, including one of the toys being a favorite for either of them, don't let that toy be part of their together time. They need to only engage with "shareable" toys while together.
- Don't let them be together unsupervised. When you are not there to keep an eye on them, keep them separated by a gate or door. Over time, let them spend longer periods of time together as they become more familiar with each other.
- Spend time with each dog individually. When you spend time with your new puppy teach them the rules of their new home. When you spend time with both of them, make sure that they are on their best behavior, and encourage each other to behave, instead of acting out.
- Don't try to force the dogs to follow your pre-planned hierarchy. While it's natural for us to think that the "older sibling" should be the leader, you should let the dogs decide this for themselves.

- If for some reason one of the dogs acts either scared or aggressive, make sure that you do not punish the other for that behavior. This means that you should be careful, especially in the moment that you do not yell, tug or push both dogs. You should calmly remove them both from the situation and correct the behavior of the dog that is wrong.

Journal Prompt

I've been encouraging you to keep a puppy journal from the day that your pup comes home, but we haven't really explored what exactly the journal will look like. Instead of going into a long-winded explanation, I'd like to give you an example of what your first-day journal entry might look like so that you have a point of reference for the rest of your pages.

Seeing my little one for the first time I felt...

_____

The first thing ___ did when they saw me was...

_____

When we got home, ___ seemed very interested in...

_____

They seemed unsure or anxious about...

_____

Their level of confidence was...

_____

Getting them to potty in the right place went like this...

_____

This should give you a general idea of the prompts and information that you should be recording in your journal. This is your baseline, but your journal is yours to create and to fill with what you feel is important about your puppy.

THREE

Command & Conquer

One of the biggest challenges humans face when it comes to the training of their canine companions is that we see training as controlling behavior. In actuality, when we train our companions, we are teaching them correct behavior. The alternative is to have them constantly engage in poor behavior that requires discipline and reprimanding. This is why a well-trained pet is happier than an untrained pet. In this chapter, we will look into the basic commands that your pet should know, and how to teach them these commands.

The Essential Basic Hand/Word Commands Every Puppy Should Know

Before we get into how to teach your puppy these commands, let's just take a moment and explore why these commands are important. I want to point out that even the order of these

commands is important as you'll see in the following section, each command is almost an extension of the previous command.

Fundamental Commands and Their Significance

While I know that teaching your dog to give you paw is all cute and a normal trick, I do want to be a bit more serious and focus more on the five essential commands that will help you guide your new friend into more acceptable behaviors.

Sit

The sit command is arguably the easiest command to teach your puppy. This is because you can be completely engaged with your puppy and guide them into this entire situation. This will help to reassure them while they start to figure out that when you make certain sounds you expect them to do certain actions. Aside from this command allowing you to reassure your puppy and make them more comfortable with following commands, this command is also quite effective at correcting behavior in various situations.

If your puppy tends to be anxious around other animals, having them sit while introducing them to another puppy can be effective in keeping them calm until they are used to the situation. The same idea applies if they tend to get too excited. Instead of them getting into the personal space of others, or causing potential harm or damage in their excitement, training them to sit until they have calmed down can help to ease any situation.

Heel

Once your pup sits on command the obvious next evolution is to get them moving. The idea of *"heel"* is to get your puppy to walk with you in a safe and controlled manner. This is extremely useful when you need to move through an area where your pup might otherwise get anxious or excited. It also helps to keep them from tugging against the leash while you are taking them for a walk.

The heel command also brings an aspect of safety to your walks. When your puppy knows to walk in a specific spot you can be assured they won't run up to other dogs who might harm them, or in the midst of their emotions run in front of a vehicle or straight into other dangers.

Stay

Being able to get your puppy to sit or walk through any situation with you is great. However, you do not always want your puppy to be part of certain situations. For example, you are trying to accept a delivery; if your puppy is in the doorway while you have your hands full and are trying to hand cash over or is trying to jump up on the delivery person, a simple delivery could turn into a nightmare. This also runs the risk of your puppy getting out for an unsanctioned run. The stay command teaches them to wait in an appropriate place until you can redirect your attention to them, or the situation has been resolved.

As a side note, this can make your vet visit a breeze. Most animals tend to get very anxious at the vet. Not just because a visit to the doctor can be scary, especially if you do not know what is going on, but there are so many new people, smells, and other animals that overwhelm pets at a veterinary office. Using the stay command can help to keep them under control so your vet has an easier time making sure your little one is safe and healthy.

Now if you can better your vet visits, where do the possibilities end?

Down

Down is an extension of both stay and sit. It can also have the same effect as both of these commands. It is especially effective in dogs that tend to get a bit aggressive when meeting other pets as it puts them in a more submissive position. That being said, you should absolutely not use the down command after your dog has started to show aggression towards other animals. This will most probably only make the situation worse.

This is also an effective command to get your puppy to learn when it is, when they should not be engaged in a situation at all, and generally when they should be calm such as when you are having dinner.

Leave

After getting the previous four commands done, the natural progression is to get your dog to drop whatever they have in their mouth. After all, your pup can easily pick anything up while walking, or chew it while sitting down and waiting for you.

The importance of the leave command is to ensure that your dog does not destroy something they are not supposed to, or worse eating something that is potentially harmful to them.

Step-By-Step Guide on Teaching These Commands To Your Puppy

Now that you understand the reason behind these five essential commands, let's get into how to teach each command to your pet. I do want to take a moment and point out that there are various different techniques teaching your puppy commands. I will be sharing with you the simplest techniques to try and help make your training journey as easy as possible.

Sit

As I've said this is the first command we'll be looking into. You'll understand soon enough why this creates the basis for all the other commands.

1. Keeping a treat in your hand, crouch down in front of your pup.
2. Touch the treat to your pup's nose.

3. Lift the treat above your pup's head. This should encourage them to lift their upper body and lower their rear. If it does not happen, you can gently push their rear side down while lifting the treat. When you push their rear down do so by gently pushing on their pelvis just above where their tail meets the body. Practicing this with your pup's behind up against a wall is sometimes helpful.

4. As soon as they are in the seated position allow them to eat the treat.

5. Repeat this process two or three times, then start repeating this without the treat. You should still reward your pup with affection and praise at this time.

6. Once your pup comfortably sits down without needing a treat or assistance from you, you can start using the verbal command "Sit" while repeating the hand motion.

7. Repeat this process until your pup responds to the verbal command without needing the hand motion.

8. Repeat the process while standing up until your dog no longer needs close contact or your reassurances.

And just like that your dog should have learned his first command. *"Sit"* is one of the easiest and fastest commands to teach your dog.

Heel

Once you have mastered sit, it's time for the heel command. Once your companion has learned to sit, they should start to follow your directions a lot more. They should by now under-

stand that your words have meaning and that you expect them to perform an action when you say something. You might notice that they start to repeat certain actions more based on your reactions. This is them trying to learn from you. So, let's learn how to get your pet to heel.

The heel command is often used in security training and dog shows. In these instances, the dog would usually walk on the left side of the handler and keep his head in line with the handler's knee. Considering we are not training your puppy for any of this, it does not matter where you prefer your pup to walk. What is important is that you remain consistent with where your puppy should walk.

1. Ensure that your puppy is comfortable with being on a leash. If they try to bite the leash or pull against it, you can give them a treat every time you put the leash on them to help them become more comfortable with it.
2. Keeping the leash in a loose loop, guide your puppy with a treat until they are in the position you want them to be when you use the heel command. Give them a few treats. Pups are smart, and this command does not usually need a verbal cue from you. Your pup will eventually learn that anytime you put the leash on them they should be in this position. However, you can use the verbal command "heel" after you place the leash on them and before you guide them to the correct position.
3. Take one step forward and encourage your pet to follow you. You can use one treat per step until they get the idea.

4. If your pup runs forward past you or moves in a different direction than you, immediately turn and walk one step in the exact opposite position of them, call them towards you, and reward them with a treat as soon as they reach the "heel" position. If you want them to use the verbal cue, this is a great time to repeat it. Make sure you repeat the command clearly and only once as you walk in the opposite direction.

5. As your pup starts to get the hang of it, start spacing out the treats. Instead of giving them a treat with each step, start giving a treat every second step, then every third, etc.

6. As you progress your pup will start staying in position longer, and eventually learn to remain in position for the entirety of the walk. Remember to let your pup explore and smell what they need to while walking with you, and to repeat the "heel" command, once you are ready to start walking again.

One of the perks of using the heel command is that once your pup has learned that it means they should walk in a certain position, you can start using it without a leash. If you do want to teach your pup how to heel without a leash, start by standing still and dropping the leash, take one step, and see if your pup follows. If they don't, repeat step 3 without picking up the leash and go from there. Keep in mind that while your pup will most likely listen to you, it is never a good idea to walk them without a leash unless you are in an area that is safe to do so, such as a secured dog park or your own property.

Stay (and Release)

Once you have gotten your new companion to follow you, it's time to do the opposite. This is usually a bit more difficult since you will now be teaching them to ignore the heel command. The reason we do stay after "heel" is that if your dog ignores the stay command, you can more easily regain control instead of having your pet running around and getting into trouble.

Before we get started, I just want to point out that this command is a two-stage command. Before we teach your pup to stay, we need to teach them when they can stop listening to you, and when they should continue following your orders. The first few steps will be about teaching your dog this release command and then working that into your stay command.

1. Choose a release command. Preferred commands are usually words like "free" or "ok." You may also use the actual word "release."
2. Use the sit command on your puppy. After your puppy has obeyed this command, throw a treat on a spot in front of them, and use your chosen command as soon as they move towards the treat. Make sure not to use the command before they move. If your pup does not move toward the treat, you can try acting as if you're about to move without actually taking a step as you throw the treat. This should encourage your pup to move.
3. Keep repeating this process until your pup easily follows the command when you give it. Then try giving the

command, and only throw the treat once your pup starts moving.

4. Keep repeating this until your pup responds to the command instead of the treat. This is the extent to which we will be teaching the release command. You can later start phasing out the treat, but I suggest we wait until at the very least after the stay command has been taught.

5. Now start teaching your pup the stay command. Give your puppy the stay command, then step in front of them facing them. Then give them a treat.

6. Wait a second or two and give them another treat if they are still seated.

7. Start waiting longer before giving a treat. A handy tip is to choose a song, a rhyme, or to just count. As you keep increasing the time between treats don't be discouraged if your pet gets up. This just means they're not ready to wait that long yet, and you need to be a bit more patient working up to that length of time.

8. Once your puppy can comfortably sit for a long period of time, think around a minute or more, you're ready for the next step.

9. While standing in front of your pup take one step backwards. As you step backward, use the "stay" command. If your pup remains seated step back towards them and give them the "release" command while giving them a treat.

10. Repeat this while gradually increasing the number of steps when you are certain your pup will stay for that amount of time.

11. Once your pup stays after a few steps, you can start taking the steps with your back towards your pup, instead of walking backward.

The stay command is especially difficult for puppies. This might take a lot of patience. Be sure you keep the training sessions for this command short. At the first sign of failure, stop the session and give your puppy time to rebuild their confidence. Just like humans, too many failures will discourage your puppy.

Down

The good news is that once your puppy has mastered the stay command, the down command will be easy. By this time your puppy should be used to learning commands from you. They will understand that your words have meaning and that you will guide them into what you need them to do. This command is also a continuation of the sit command and can be used for the stay command as well.

1. Use the sit command on your puppy. Once they are seated touch a treat to their nose and use the "down" command while lowering the treat all the way to the floor.
2. Remember that your pup will now need to learn that you are guiding them into another command, by using a previous command. So do not be discouraged if they do not get it completely right the first few times. You can give them the treat when their elbows touch the ground.

3. Continue this, while waiting to give your pup the treat until they are lower than the previous time.

4. Once your pup repeatedly gets into a laying down position, repeat the hand action without a treat in your hand. Remember to use the verbal command as well. Just like with the sit command start weaning them off the treats.

5. Once your pup follows your hand command without requiring a treat, you can start to issue only the verbal command without the hand command and give them a treat when they respond to the verbal command, while again weaning them off the treats.

Down is fairly easy to learn, if you want your pup to stay in a down position, remember to practice this first and to treat it as if you are teaching them a new command at first.

Leave It

The final command we'll look into is the leave command. This is an extremely important command for when your pup gets hold of something they shouldn't have. This, of course, includes every-thing from your favorite pair of shoes to your electric appliances, to the piece of food that they stole off the counter when your back was turned. Another perk of the leave command is that teaching it can be quite fun.

1. You'll need two treats. Place one on the ground but cover it so that your puppy cannot get it to, but still smell it. Keep the other treat in your hand.

2. Wait until your pup loses interest in the covered treat. When they do so, immediately use the "leave it". Give them the treat in your hand immediately.

3. Repeat this until your puppy loses interest in the covered treat faster. Then start to try and use the command before your pup loses interest. If they immediately disengage from the treat, then you can reward them. Otherwise, wait until they disengage and use the command.

4. Once your pup starts responding to the command, you can make it more difficult by leaving the treat on the ground uncovered.

While this can be a fun command to learn, it can also be difficult. Your pup is used to a treat being a reward, so they will not understand that they are not allowed to take this treat at first. Remember to not be too harsh on them, and to not allow them to fail too often.

Positive Training

Positive training is extremely important for any pup. As I've said before, pups can be just like humans. If they see something as a negative experience, they are less likely to engage with it.

One of the best ways to ensure that their training sessions are not negative experiences is to use positive reinforcement in order to help them learn. When we give them a treat when they successfully obey a command or partake in behavior, we want them to repeat, we are actively practicing positive reinforcement.

Some people see positive reinforcement as being a bribe, instead of actually training your pet. This is completely incorrect. Remember a bribe is something that you need to receive each time you take a certain action, training teaches you to do the action, even if you do not always get rewarded for it. This is why we wean our pups off the treat when we are training them.

While positive reinforcement goes a long way to making your training a happy experience for your companion, there are some other tricks you can use to make the sessions go a lot smoother.

- You should be having fun yourself. Remember that your pet will pick up on your mood, if you feel negative about the situation, chances are they will as well. So, make sure that you smile and have fun as well.
- Make it a game. When you are playing a game with your pet, you are laughing, and giving them more attention and a positive atmosphere than you might realize. So wherever possible, try to add a game component to your training session. For example, when you teach your dog to stay, after a while you can start hiding around a corner, or behind objects. When you give the release command, your pet will automatically search for you, and you can reward them with a playful display of affection when they find you. Coincidentally, this is also very similar to the techniques that are used to teach dogs how to use their nose to find people and objects, so your companion might pick up a handy new skill without even trying.

- Don't push too hard. By keeping your daily training sessions short and sweet, and not pushing your pet past their limits, you make this an activity that they look forward to while giving them enough time afterward to relax and recover from any failure they may have faced.
- Don't stress the oopsies. Seriously, when something goes wrong, just take it in stride. When you start to worry too much about their failures, your pet will pick up on that added stress. In turn, this will make the training session more difficult for them.

Common Mistakes to Avoid and Tips for Success

Mistakes are bound to happen, everyone makes them. In a moment I'll share a story with you to prove this. However, for now, we'll look into the most common mistakes we tend to make when it comes to training, and how to avoid them.

Getting a Late Start

This is perhaps the most common mistake. When we get a new pup, we often want to give them some time to get used to their new environment and family before we start training them. While this is admirable and completely understandable, it's also very counterproductive. While I'm not suggesting that you try and get your pup to heel on the first day of his arrival, some basic rules and guidance is important. Start with things like potty training and work your way up as they become ready for more complicated behavior like sitting.

Spending the Wrong Amount of Time on Training

Life is busy and difficult. During the week we are generally busy with work and all our adult responsibilities. At night we are exhausted and need time to unwind. Weekends are equally busy. This is when we do everything that we don't have time for during the week.

Herein lies the problem. We tend to not spend enough time every day training our pets, and then over weekends or free days, we try and spend the entire day training which results in over-working our pups.

The only way to not make this mistake is to set a proper training schedule that allows short training sessions each day. This is a major responsibility, so make sure you are up for it.

Training Anywhere

While it is true that your pup needs to learn how to act in any environment, their training should not occur in just any environment. The mistake people often make in this regard is to try and train their puppy in an environment that is not supportive of their training.

As we learned in Chapter 1, each puppy responds to stimuli in a different way. You need to learn what stimuli are conducive to your pup's training, and what is counterproductive. Take special care in deciding where to train your puppy.

Reinforcing Bad Behavior

This is often done without even realizing it. Think of when a puppy begs for some human food, it's so easy to give in to those eyes. The problem is that when you give in, you reward that type of behavior.

When your puppy engages in poor behavior you might think that the best thing to do is whatever it takes to get them to stop this behavior. This, however, is when we tend to make the most mistakes. When you take your pup out for potty, and they don't do their business right away, you might think the best thing to do is to bring them back in. Then they end up going potty inside the house. The correct response would be to wait until they eventually finish their potty business outside and to possibly refresh the schedule as to which you are taking them outside.

Repeating Command Cues

When we are trying to teach our puppy something and they don't immediately get it, we often think that by repeating the command until the puppy does what is expected of them, we are helping them. In actuality, this confuses them.

Have you ever tried to speak to someone who is talking in a completely different language? The same applies to your puppy. They won't understand what is required of them, all they see is someone repeating the same words over and over, and eventually, they get a treat.

This is why it is extremely important to only use the command once. If your puppy does not respond to it, don't simply repeat the command, but take a step back and use a treat to show your puppy what you need them to do.

Getting Emotional

Yes, we all tend to get frustrated when things do not go as planned. This includes training your puppy. When you get frustrated, your puppy picks up on these emotions. They start to feel like they are doing something wrong, and their training session becomes a negative experience.

Aside from your pet picking up on these emotions, we tend to make more mistakes and act unfairly towards others when we are frustrated. This can cause you to easily lose patience or be too harsh on your puppy when they make a mistake. When a situation escalates in this manner, it can cause your puppy to completely reject any attempt at training.

If you start to get frustrated with the training, the best option is to stop the session for the day, and perhaps look into your training techniques and see if there are any changes you can make to create a more positive experience for yourself and your pup.

What Type Of Trainer Are You Quiz

Let's look at what type of trainer you are. This quiz will help you determine the approach you are most likely to take to training, and in doing so will help you to identify what you need to give attention to when it comes to training.

Question 1

Which of these best describes you as a trainer?

A. I'm the trainer here. When I say something, don't ask me why, just do it.

B. Training is a journey meant to be done together. When my dog respects me, he will cooperate with me.

C. My puppy needs to learn at their own pace. I'll try and teach them, but if they don't look into it, we'll try again tomorrow.

Question 2

What is your motivation for training your pet?

A. My dog should be obedient and have respect for others.

B. It's a bonding exercise and will help us get along better.

C. It's something we can do together, and it's totally cool to show off what they can do.

Question 3

How patient are you when it comes to training?

A. I like it when things go my way immediately.

B. Mistakes are going to happen. We'll catch them in stride and learn from them.

C. Mistakes happen, when they do it's generally a good place to stop for the day.

Question 4

When a mistake inevitably occurs, what is your reaction?

A. Correct it immediately. Discipline my pet if needed.

B. Let's analyze where it went wrong and how we can avoid that in the future.

C. Mistakes happen, let's take a breath, play a bit, and maybe we'll come back to training today.

Question 5

What tools do you use during training?

A. Any tools I can find. This includes correction tools like choke chains. If they don't hurt, they are useful.

B. Affection, treats, clickers, and any other positive reinforcement tools I can find.

C. Just affection. Treats are bribing, and clickers don't work.

Question 6

How much time do you spend on training each day?

A. As much time as possible.

B. We have a certain block of time reserved each day for training. It's the same amount every time.

C. Whenever I have a few minutes to spare.

Question 7

How do you feel about crates?

A. They're great. Especially for time-outs!

B. My pet has a crate for themselves. They can use it whenever they need to feel safe, or I need to ensure they are safe.

C. My pet does not know what a crate is, my space is their space.

Question 8

How do you determine whether your dog is succeeding or not?

A. They do as I command sometimes before I even think of which command to give them.

B. They follow my commands, but they also know how to communicate with me when they cannot or will not for whatever reason.

C. My pup is happy.

Results

So, to see what the answer is, let's add up the total of your answers using the following scoring system.

All "A" answers get five points.
All "B" answers get three points.
All "C" answers get two points.

21–24 points mean you are the drill sergeant. You are strict and know what results you want as well as when to get them. You will accept nothing short of perfection. The problem here is that you might overwork your pup or turn training sessions into negative experiences. Try to relax a little and have some fun with it.

14–20 points mean that you are the yin and yang of training. Perfect balance. However, this balance is difficult to keep. Be careful and keep an eye on your approach, keep it balanced as you go. You've got this.

8–13 points suggest you're the chilled buddy. You might be trying to do some training, but without a bit more effort and structure, you won't be getting far. Your problem is most probably those puppy eyes or the human-like hugs. Don't be scared of taking charge a bit, I promise you that you won't hurt them or make your pup miserable.

Results

So to see what the answer is, let's add... up for each of your... level totaling the following scoring system:

    all A answers get no points.
    all B answers get one points.
    all C answers get two points.

0-3 points: With you and the dull sergeant, you're doing fine and... know what really you... And what's... when it... us about you... all appropriate... be? Be certain that the well-rested... you might overwork your body or turn you're a schedule into... negative experiences. Try to relax a little... and have all of... that it...

4-8 points: more than volume, the dull well-rested... healthy... proper balance. However, they have a significant to keep the... careful and learn to relax... approach help you enjoy all of... and with your activities.

9-15 points: Answer says it's quite... you... wanting to do something of... but without a bit more effort and attention, you won't maximize the... You... reaching... to the Sunshine... things. Don't be scared to... fall the... hope a bit, promises... that you will want from them or... make you happier and...

FOUR

Positive Paws

We've talked a lot about positive reinforcement, but there is always more to discover. This chapter is specifically meant to focus on positive reinforcement so that you can understand why pups respond better after being rewarded for good behavior, instead of being punished for bad behavior.

Benefits of Positive Reinforcement in Puppy Training

To understand positive reinforcement better, we need to explore how this technique can be more beneficial compared to negative reinforcement. By understanding the benefits, we can understand why we use this method.

With positive reinforcement, you and your furball start to learn how to communicate with each other. Without even realizing you are both creating a language that you two understand. This

language is based on trust and mutual respect. When a trainer uses negative reinforcement, their pet becomes fearful of them, and the relationship can become unhealthy. Think of it this way, are you more inclined to have a conversation with the friend that celebrates your success with you, or the friend that points out all your failures along the way?

So, our first benefit is that you and your pet will be able to understand each other.

This leads us to the next point, through positive reinforcement your bond with your pet is strengthened. This is because your pet knows that when they make a mistake you are more than likely to be there for them and to help them turn it into a positive experience, and if you can turn their own mistakes into positive experiences, what would you do when they don't even make mistakes? So, when they get hurt, or they feel threatened, they understand you are a safe zone and they can find comfort and protection from you.

This means that our second benefit is that you and your pet will enjoy a strong bond that will lead to a lot of affection and loyalty.

Now I want you to think about a situation that you tend to feel negatively about. Let's say a previous job you had where your manager was an absolute nightmare. How often did you feel bored there? Not because you had nothing to do, but because what you were doing was no longer stimulating you in a positive manner. The same idea goes for your pet. When they have a "*Meanager*" they won't be enjoying their training sessions. The result of this would be that they tend to experience boredom

more, and when a pet is bored, they act out. So, say goodbye to your favorite pair of shoes!

This benefit is that your pet will be less likely to engage in negative behaviors such as chewing on items they are not supposed to be chewing or ignoring their potty training.

Additionally, your pet also learns behavior from you. Negative reinforcement is rooted in negative behavior and emotions. When a pet does something wrong, they are met with anger and criticism. The biggest problem with this is that when you start the training, your pet will do something "wrong" since they do not yet know what the right thing to do is. This means that your pet will learn from you not to be patient and wait for someone else to learn what the right thing is, but to instead snap at the first mistake someone makes. This can be a dangerous trait for any pet to have.

The last benefit to keep in mind is that your pet will have more patience and in general a more positive demeanor toward others. Remember, there are many more benefits that have not been included here that you will still discover for yourself.

As you can see, there is a huge difference between positive and negative reinforcement. The manner in which you choose to train your pet has a deep impact, not just on their ability to learn, but also on their entire identity.

I also want to take a moment to talk about some of the tools of negative reinforcement. Specifically, tools like choke chains and shock collars. There are many people who swear by these tools. They will tell you that these tools are completely safe and that

your pet will not be harmed. "There is almost no pain, the dog gets more of a fright than hurt." is a line that I've heard repeated far too often. While I won't be arguing the truth behind these statements, I do want you to think about one thing when considering whether or not to use correctional tools. What is the worst way in which it can go wrong? Is it worth risking your pet on Murphy's whims?

Practical Examples and Techniques for Implementing Positive Reinforcement

So far, I've been focusing on using treats and to some point affection as part of your positive reinforcement techniques. But these are not your only options. They are simply the options to which most people have access, and which work the best. Now I'd like to look into more options that are available to you.

Let's start off with dog toys. Think of a ball, a rope, or any other toy you can find at your local vet that is approved for use with your furry friend. The reason why people often choose to use toys instead of treats is that toys encourage exercise, agility, and good health. Whereas treats can quite easily lead to gluttony and an unhealthy diet.

The main problem with toys is that dogs don't always like to play with toys, or, they like them so much that they lose their minds completely. Luckily this behavior can also be influenced and changed as needed. If your dog does not like to engage with toys in any way, it's actually quite simple to get them to start enjoying the toys. You just need to enjoy the toys yourself. No, really. If you get excited about something, your cute companion will too.

Be as silly as you can and move and play with that toy as much as you can while giving your pupper more than enough chance to join in on the fun.

On the other hand, if your pup gets too excited with toys, you can limit their exposure and time with the "read toy." This will be done in a similar way as to when you are trying to get your pet to start playing with a toy. Make sure you are engaged in the play with your pet, and that you keep a certain amount of control over the toy. Don't allow your pet to run off and go too crazy. Instead, allow them to play for a little bit, and then calmly and gently disengage the play and take the toy away. This will give them even more reason to follow your commands since they so sorely want this toy again.

Up next, we have clickers. While we will have a deeper look into clickers in a later chapter, it's still important to note them here. Clickers are not a reward in themselves at first. Instead, they are part of conditioning your dog to know they are being rewarded. We will get into the specifics later. A clicker is traditionally used with treats in the beginning and offers an affordable and calmer way of practicing positive reinforcement. You don't need as much space or money to replace toys and treats when you are using a clicker.

Up next, we have play as a reward. While this sounds like it is the same thing as using a toy, it's not. When you are using the toy as a reward, it is their interaction with the toy that is what shows them they did something correctly. When you are using play as a reward it is the interaction with you specifically that is their reward. This is when you allow them to have a physical interac-

tion with you without having anything else in between. For example, when you teach them the stay command, once you give them the release command you allow them to run towards you and chase you a bit before they "catch" you. This technique allows you to build an even stronger bond with your pet. The downside is that you often need a lot of space, and that this technique tends to hype your pet up quite a lot, which can make it more difficult to get back into the training mindset. However, some dogs not only prefer this technique but might require it.

I would also like to take a moment and visit the praise technique as well. This is quite similar to the play technique, but instead of going crazy and building up as much energy as playing does. You quite calmly reward your pet by petting them, rubbing them, or giving them affection in whichever other way you deem fit. You can even just use some encouraging words in a happy and excited tone of voice. The benefit to this is that your dog tends to over-react far less than with any other technique, and you don't need to spend money in any way.

Lastly, I also need to clarify some points when it comes to using treats as a reward. You already know how it works, but the question is still there, what treats do you use? How many do you give them? What size? Etcetera.

The key is to use small treats, you don't want your pet to overindulge. They also need to be easily hidden so that your pet does not get distracted by them. Make sure these treats are tasty and that your furball really loves them. They need to want them to see them as a reward. That being said, make sure you change the treats often. Do not let your pet become used to, and in doing

so, get bored with the treats, this will diminish the effectiveness of the treat as a reward.

While positive reinforcement does not have as many options available to you as negative reinforcement does, you don't need that many options because these options are extremely effective.

Building a Strong Bond With Your Puppy

Training your pet is not just about ensuring they have good manners. It is about building a relationship with your newest family member. Positive reinforcement is one of the best ways to do this. As we've already seen, it does create a strong, positive, and healthy bond between the two of you.

I've mentioned several times that this bond creates a type of communication between you and your puppy. But what does that actually mean? Of course, you won't know what your puppy is trying to say specifically. Instead, you will better learn to know what your dog is feeling, or what their plans or thoughts are at the moment.

For example, how do you know when your pet has a stomach ache? This isn't something they can outright tell you, or that has physical symptoms you can see. Some pets continue to eat while they have stomach aches, while others stop eating immediately. There are also many other reasons why pets could stop eating. When you have a strong bond with your puppy you will notice the subtle changes in their behavior, and without realizing it you might just start wondering if maybe their stomach is upset. And there you have it, communication without even trying.

When it comes to the loyalty aspect of this bond you might be thinking that your pet will be loyal to you regardless of your aspect. That is just the nature of any dog. While this is true, the level of loyalty differs based on your bond. For example, if your pet doesn't really trust you or have any positive relationship with you, their loyalty might easily shift. It can easily mean the difference between your pet betraying you for another family member, running away when you are being threatened by someone, turning on you themselves, or being your ride or die.

This is the importance of the bond. Additionally, this bond will determine how likely your little creature is to take guidance and direction from you. The stronger the bond, the more likely your pet is to listen to you and to want to do whatever it takes to make you happy. Including learning new tricks and behaviors.

The close bond that you form with your pet through positive reinforcement cannot be replicated with any other type of training or lack thereof.

Positive Reinforcement Tracker

Below is a printable document that you can use in your puppy journal to track the positive reinforcement you use and how effective it is. The document is fairly easy to use. You simply need to fill in the date and time of when the reward and behavior occurred. Explain what behavior they engaged in that required a reward, such as using the correct place to go to the bathroom, or being calm and on their best behavior when a visitor came in. Then it is followed by what reward you gave them, for example giving them a treat and verbal praise. Finally, you will add in

your notes about the event. Your notes will help give extra information such as saying you didn't need to give a command for it to occur, or this is new behavior that they are learning, or perhaps this behavior came with a struggle and needs to be reinforced more often.

Date	Time	Behavior Description	Reward Given	Notes

Transform Puppy Chaos with Your Review

EMBRACE THE MAGIC OF PAWSITIVITY

"Kindness is like a tail wag - it brings joy wherever it goes."

Furry Wisdom

People who share their knowledge and experiences not only make the world a better place but also find joy and fulfillment in doing so. So, let's embark on a journey together to spread the love for our furry friends.

To make that happen, I have a simple request for you...

Would you lend a paw to a fellow puppy owner, even if you never received a treat for it?

Who is this person you wonder? They are just like you or, at least, like you were before becoming a pro puppy trainer. Eager to make a difference, in need of guidance, and unsure where to find it.

Our mission is to make the journey of puppy training accessible to everyone, and your review is a paw-some contribution to achieving that. You see, most people judge a book by its reviews, and here's my heartfelt ask on behalf of a struggling puppy owner you've never met:

Please lend a paw by leaving a review for this book.

Your gift costs no money and takes less than 60 seconds, but it can change a fellow puppy owner's life forever. Your review might help...

...one more family enjoy the antics of their playful pup.

...one more pup find their forever home.

...one more person discover the joy of training a furry friend.

To leave your review, simply scan the QR code:

If the thought of helping a faceless puppy owner warms your heart, welcome to our pack. You're officially one of us!

We're thrilled to share the secrets of successful puppy training that will make your journey easier and more rewarding than you can imagine. The lessons in this book are like little treats for your training toolbox.

Thank you from the bottom of our hearts! Now, let's get back to creating a world where every puppy is a well-trained superstar!

- Your biggest fans, F&F

PS - Did you know? Providing value to others makes you more valuable to them. If you think this book can help another puppy enthusiast, share the love. After all, sharing is caring!

FIVE

Clicker Crusader

We've touched on clickers a bit throughout the guide so far, now as promised it's time to understand how clicker training works, and why dogs that are trained with a clicker tend to learn commands 50% faster than those trained with only verbal praise.

Introduction to Clicker Training and Its Benefits

I want you to do an exercise. Don't worry, it's nothing too difficult. I want you to take a pen, and your cellphone and go stand in the mall. Play a podcast or some video that includes only someone talking, then keep the phone and pen at equal distances in opposite directions away from you and click the pen a few times while the video plays on the other side. Which is easier, to hear the click of the pen, or to identify each word, as well as the emotion behind them on the video?

You see this is why a clicker is so effective. It is a strong, constant sound that is easily identified between other sounds. Whereas verbal praise is difficult to identify. Your pet might not always be able to hear you very well, and your tone of voice will change every day based on what is happening in your own life. This means that while you might be trying to sound happy and positive, you will sometimes not be able to do that very well. This can become confusing to your pet and make it difficult for him to understand what is happening.

So, what exactly is a clicker, and how do dogs get rewards from them? Well, a clicker is exactly what you think. It's a little toy that makes a distinct clicking noise when you press it. There is nothing special about it. The magic is in how you turn it into a reward for your pet. We'll get to a step-by-step guide on how to do this in a moment, but essentially the click is initially followed by a treat. This will teach your pet that when they hear the clicking sound, they did something right and will be rewarded for it. Eventually, they become conditioned to associate the click with doing the correct thing. So, while they might not receive the reward immediately anymore, they still know that the click means they did something right.

Of course, the clicker won't always be needed. After some time, the clicker can be taken away once your pet has learned the behavior you wanted to teach them, and only be brought out again when they need to be refreshed.

Clicker training comes with its own set of benefits as well. Thanks to the consistency of the clicker, it tends to help build up their confidence a lot better and faster. This is due to the fact that

if they don't hear a click, they don't feel like they did something wrong. They know they just need to keep trying until they get it right.

This also means that the bond between you and your pup is strengthened a lot faster. We've already covered what this bond is and what it means, so I won't get into it again.

A clicker also adds structure to your dog's routine. Once your dog learns that certain behavior is followed by a click which is followed by a reward, then they will be eager to engage in any behavior that fits into this formula. This means that they will look forward to their training sessions and want to participate in them. This makes following a training schedule a lot easier.

This desire will also encourage them to learn, and in doing so, make training of new behavior faster and easier. In fact, your pet will take the initiative. They will start to try and find ways to solve problems on their own. Of course, this will be done in search of more rewards. This is achieved thanks to the fact that the clicker and the positive reinforcement that comes with it are actually fun for your dog.

How to Incorporate Clicker Training Into Your Training Routine

Now that you have a better understanding of what the clicker is, and how it works, let's see how we can implement it in your routine.

A Step-By-Step Guide to Introducing Your Puppy to the Clicker

Before we look into the clicker any further, let's look at how to implement a clicker in our training routine. We'll use the sit command as an example for this scenario.

1. Start off in a quiet and private space. You need your furball's undivided attention. Introduce them to the clicker by clicking it, and then immediately give them a treat until they start to associate the sound of the clicker with getting a treat. Normally this would be when they look to your hand with the treat immediately once they hear the click.
2. Now take it into the training field. When your puppy sits down, immediately click the clicker, and then give them a treat. You might need to encourage your puppy to sit down until they learn that whenever they sit, they get a click and treat.
3. Now start adding your verbal commands. When your puppy sits down, say "sit" and then click and treat.
4. Once your puppy has learned to associate the word with the action and the reward, you can try giving them the command first, and if they oblige, give them a click and treat.
5. Once your puppy starts obeying the command, you can start phasing out the click-and-treat reward until they completely respond to the verbal cue without needing a click-and-treat afterward.

As with anything else, there are always some mistakes that can be made and misconceptions that can find their way to us. When it comes to using clickers, there are three common mistakes that new trainers tend to make. The first is using the clicker to get your pet's attention, instead of only using it as a reward. The reason for this is two-fold. First, it's easy to just click it a few times, especially once your dog associates it with a treat because then they are always listening for it.

The second is that there have been so many instances of reality shows showing clickers being used to grab attention, instead of a reward, that the general public has started to think of this as acceptable. The problem with using your clicker for attention is that it confuses your pet. When they hear the click, they think they did something correct and will be rewarded with it. So, they'll repeat whatever behavior they were busy with when they received the click in hopes of receiving their treat as they usually do.

This brings us to the second most common mistake, which is poor treat delivery. This is when the click is not always followed by a treat or too much time has passed before your pet received their treat. This can also include using treats that are not as enticing to your dog. The issue with this mistake is that your pet won't feel properly rewarded. When they are not properly rewarded, they will not be properly motivated. This will mean that they will be less likely to take the initiative or want to seek out new positive behavior.

The final mistake that is made is assuming that all dogs are only motivated by food and that the clicker can only be paired with edible rewards. As we've seen in the previous chapter, other rewards can be a part of positive reinforcement. The clicker can be followed by a reward such as a toy or affection. Treats and food do not need to be your only form of reward.

Aside from these mistakes, there are also some common misconceptions regarding clickers that we need to look into. The first of these misconceptions is that all these treats will make your dog fat. While your dog will be ingesting a lot more food, you can easily adjust their diet to make up for these nutritional additions. The idea is also not to give your dog so many treats that they ingest more treats than food. If you find yourself giving them an excess number of treats, you are either giving too often, or your pet is succeeding in their training and it is time for you to start weaning them off these treats for whatever command you are currently teaching them.

The second major misconception is that only dogs that are easy to train can be trained using a clicker. The reason behind this misconception is that clickers make training so easy that people think it's the dog that is easy and not the routine that makes the dog easy. It's the perfect example of results being so good that it cannot be believed.

The final misconception is that clicker training is only used for teaching tricks, and not for more serious training such as discipline. The misconception stems from the idea that anything fun cannot be serious. Clicker training tends to be seen as soft, fun, happy, and extremely gentle. So how can it be used to teach dogs

something serious and difficult such as obedience? Well, there's not much I can say other than not everything needs to be serious and difficult all the time, and that if you don't believe me the best way to prove either one of us right and the other wrong, is to test it out.

Professional Opinions

I'd like to tell you a story. This is the story of a border collie named Jack. I found this story on the Karen Pryor clicker training website (Premaza, 2023). As always, the link to the original story can be found in the reference section.

You see Jack was a rescue puppy in a shelter, up until he was about three months old. That's when he was finally adopted. Unfortunately for the next 11 months of his life, he suffered with this family. When he didn't respond correctly to commands, he would be hit over the head. He would be chained up outside without water for hours or be locked in his crate in the basement whenever there were visitors, or the family felt he was being too much for them.

This kind of abusive treatment does nothing other than condone further negative and abusive behavior, but this time from the dogs themselves. This was evident in Jack. He soon started to act aggressively and would snap at people for a variety of reasons. Most often when someone would attempt to touch him.

Luckily, the right person found their way into Jack's life. Pretty soon, he was rehomed and lived on a farm where his healing could finally begin. However, this wasn't without its challenges.

Jack's new mom got him into training classes. At first, this didn't go too well, and Jack's issues were immediately apparent. The trainer agreed to take Jack for one-on-one sessions and Jack was quickly introduced to a clicker and its benefits.

When the one-on-one sessions began, the trainer used a combination of tools, including a fake hand, to start getting Jack used to the touch of a human. This of course didn't go without a bit of trouble. But by the end of the first session, Jack no longer became aggressive immediately when someone touched his collar. He, of course, still did not like it, but there was some progress.

Over the next few months, the trainer and Jack's mom took their time. They had to keep Jack muzzled for most of the time, while the trainer would click the clicker and Jack's mom would supply him with the treat immediately. Slowly, they started to get him used to touching, then hugging, and even more physical interaction with time. While during training they were taking steps to allow the biggest of challenges to be overcome, at home Jack's mom had smaller challenges to focus on.

Jack needed medication in his ear every day. The problem was that Jack hated if anyone got near his ears. Using the clicker, his mom slowly got him used to allowing someone near his ears. Eventually, she managed to get him to allow her to actually put the medication in his ears without him trying to sink his teeth into her. She even managed to do this without needing any assistance from the trainer.

The progress that Jack had started to make thanks to his training and the trusty clicker he had learned to love, started to show. Jack became used to physical interactions, enough that he could

finally be groomed. His mom could use a comb on him, and his coat started to look good. Aside from the physical improvements, there were emotional improvements. While he would initially lie down and glare at his new family like a bald eagle at some tasty little fishy, after a while, his eyes started to soften. Instead of the glare, his look started to convey love and trust.

As his behavior and trust started to improve, he allowed his new mom to take his training further out of his comfort zone. Eventually, she could take him to the dog park and start to get him used to other dogs. In fact, Jack had made so much progress that when his new mom accidentally messed up and took him for his first socializing session at a dog park with narrow roads, at the busiest time of the day, it went without incident. It wasn't easy, but considering the blunder and how bad it could have gone, it went quite well.

It took about two years, and that wasn't the end of it. The damage done to Jack in the first year of his life was too much. There are some things that will stick with him for the rest of his life. However, by the end of the two years when the story was written, Jack was able to allow strangers to touch him, he allowed strangers in the car with his mom, and would no longer get aggravated over any interaction, and he even stopped guarding any object he believed to belong to him with that same level of total aggression.

In this story, you can see that not only did Jack's forever mom discover the benefits of clicker training to the point that she no longer leaves the home without the clicker, but she was taught so by a trainer who understood the value of using a clicker. This

story is also an example that with love, consistency, and positive reinforcement, even the harsh and serious nature of life can be faced head-on, and successfully.

The Clicker Community

Unlike in the other chapters, this time I don't have an interactive element like a journal prompt. Instead, I would like to encourage you to join a community.

You see, puppy training is not just about you and your puppy. It is about those around you as well. It ensures that your pup can interact with others and that you both can have a life outside of the confines of the four walls you live in. This is easily achieved in this modern age of social media.

The first suggestion I would make is to find clubs around you. Use your local Facebook group and look for signs at the local dog park. Talk to your friends who also have dogs and find out if you have any clubs in your area that serve as support groups for dog owners who are training their dogs. While it is generally difficult to find communities in person that specialize in one specific type of training, you might be able to find trainers using the same techniques as you in other dog groups. Even if they don't use the exact same technique, you will be able to find companionship with someone who understands your woes, and who can have constructive conversations with you regarding your training techniques.

While in-person groups are preferable, the internet has a wealth of resources if you know where to look. Unfortunately, these groups are not too easy to find. If you join communities like the American Kennel Club, however, you will have your foot in the door and know where to start looking. There are also online forums such as gundogforum.com. While this might not be exactly the right forum for you, they do have conversations regarding topics that might interest you, and in these conversations, you can also find directions to more suitable forums.

SIX

Crate Kingdom

Crates can be a controversial subject. A lot of people believe them to be inhumane and restrictive. As we read in Jack's story, this can be true. Then again, so can a bedroom if used maliciously. I want you to think about the crate as your pup's bedroom. You are not confining your pup when you use a crate, you are instead giving them a safe space to use and retreat to as and when they want to, or when it is necessary for their safety and wellbeing.

The Importance of Crate Training and How it Can Benefit Both You and Your Puppy

Have you ever noticed that dogs seem to like sleeping in corners, against the wall, on a small pillow, heck they are the happiest when they stretch out their bodies against the confines of their small doggy bed. Have you ever wondered why that is?

There is actually science behind this. Going all the way back to their genealogy from wolves. You see, while wolves make their home on grass, they also like to sleep under leaves and in bushes. But the reason they enjoy these confined spaces goes back to how wolves are born. They are usually born inside a den. This is a natural instinct to protect them from other predators until they are grown enough to look after themselves.

While I've already said that dogs are not wolves, and they don't live by the same rules anymore, there are still some instincts that are left over from their ancestry. While they no longer feel the need to hide in a den, they still like the confined spaces as it makes them feel secure. Now look at a crate. What is it, if not a larger above-ground den?

The safety and security that dogs feel in a crate can be handy in a variety of situations. When they feel threatened or scared, this is a spot where they can go to where they can be assured of their own safety. This allows them to disengage from a situation before it becomes too much for them. They can also use their crate to relax and get rid of negative emotions such as stress.

In an emergency, a crate can actually save your pup's life. If your dog is properly trained, they will retreat to the crate whenever they feel unsafe. This makes it easy for you to find them if anything goes wrong, or for you to direct emergency responders to where they can find your pet if you cannot get to them yourself. I know of some parents who have gone as far as to paint markers on their floors for emergency responders to know that there is a pet and where to find them.

Crates can also have medical benefits for dogs. For example, there may be times after your dog has visited the vet that they will need to take it easy. This can be due to them having stitches that could tear, muscles and ligaments that need to heal, or any other sort of injury that should not be aggravated. A crate can help to ensure they don't move around or engage in any activity that could cause more damage.

Of course, there are times when you will need to guide your pet into the crate, even when they don't feel the need to be in there. I'm not talking about crating them when you have visitors just so they don't annoy you. I'm talking about crating them when there is a potentially dangerous situation for them, or when you might not be around to supervise them. Just keep in mind that it's not healthy to keep your dog in the crate all night while you sleep, and then all day while you are at work. Just like humans, dogs also need to exercise and stretch their legs regularly throughout the day.

Finally, if your pup happens to be a rescue. A crate might be their favorite possession. In the rescue center, your puppy most probably didn't have their own toys and had to share their kennel with other dogs. Now, they'll have a crate that is completely their own. No other dogs or humans will enter this space. This will not only make them feel more welcome and secure, but happier and safer as well.

A Step-By-Step Guide on How to Crate Train Your Puppy

As you've no doubt realized by now, we'll have a step-by-step guide for you to make sure that you can easily introduce crating to your pup's life.

1. Start by introducing your pup to their crate. This is done by first placing the crate in a space your family uses often like the living room.
2. Make the crate comfortable for your pet. Add a blanket, a doggy bed, a pillow, or anything that will make the space warm and comfortable for your pet.
3. Start bringing your pup closer to the crate. Encourage them to move closer to it on their own, and relax them by talking with them in soothing tones, and calmly petting them.
4. Place a reward like a treat or a toy just inside the opening of the crate to encourage your pup to start moving in. Remember even though they enjoy these spaces, it can still be scary at first. If your pup is scared of going in, move the reward to as close to the opening as your pup is willing to go, and systematically move it closer until you can get it to the inside of the opening.
5. Once your pup starts getting more comfortable around the crate you can start feeding them as deep into the crate as they are comfortable. Slowly move their bowls deeper into the crate until they are comfortable eating all the way in the back of the crate.
6. Once your pup is completely inside the crate, gently and slowly close the gate behind them while they are eating.

As soon as your pup finishes their meal, open the crate and let them out.

7. As your pup starts to get used to the crate being closed, start keeping it closed longer. Take this process as slowly as possible, and don't leave your pup alone in there while they are still getting comfortable.

8. Once your puppy is comfortable with the crate being closed for longer periods it's time to start teaching your pup that it's okay for them to be in the crate alone.

9. The next time you lead your pup to the crate, use a command cue such as "crate" or "kennel" when they go into the crate, followed by your choice of positive reinforcement.

10. Close the door, give them another treat, and move a small distance away from the crate. Keep repeating this until you can get all the way to the door without your dog becoming distressed.

11. Next, you will start leaving them alone in the room. Start with thirty seconds, then a minute, and keep gradually increasing the time. Make sure every time you get back into the room, you immediately release them from the crate.

12. You can start going on short errands once your pup is easily comfortable with at least thirty minutes. In time you can start to increase the time you are out little by little.

13. Before you go on long errands, place your pup in their crate a few minutes before you leave. Anything from 5 minutes to 15 minutes should be fine.

14. When you leave the home, do so with a purpose. Do not linger, do not stand at the door and coo for too long. Simply walk out and say goodbye as you would to any normal loved one.

15. When you return from wherever you were, walk directly to the crate, open your pup, and greet your pup as you would greet any other person. Do not make it a big deal. Remember your pup will match your energy.

That's the basics of crate training. Make sure that you also crate your puppy sometimes while you are at home during their training days so they understand that just because they are in the crate, it does not mean that they are completely alone.

Tips for Creating a Comfortable and Safe Crate Environment for Your Puppy

There are several aspects to look into when choosing a crate for your pet. You need to ensure that the crate actually offers your pet enough safety while being comfortable enough for them to call it their own space.

The first step in doing so is to find a crate that is the perfect size. Think of your pet as Goldilocks chose a bed. You can't get one that is too big, because then your pet might see it as just another room, and end up relieving themselves in there, and not feeling too secure. You also can't get one that is too small, since your furry friend will not feel comfortable in there. Instead, have your companion stand normally, and then measure from the tip of his

tail to the tip of his nose, and from the floor to the top of the highest point of his body, whether this is his tail in the air, his ears, or the top of his back. Now add about four inches to each measurement, and you should have the perfect size for your pet's crate.

Next, you will need to choose the type of crate. You have a few options to choose from. Plastic, metal, wood, and fabric. Each type of crate has its pros and cons. So don't feel like you have to choose a certain type of crate because that is what people usually choose. It is up to you to decide what is right for you and your furry family member.

- **material:** These crates are made from fabric. They tend to be the most affordable types of crates, but that affordability comes at a price. They are less durable than any other type of crate. These crates are soft and as such are more likely to be chewed or destroyed by pups that still enjoy their teeth too much. The perk is that these crates can also be used as travel crates and can easily be set up anywhere you need them.
- **plastic:** These are great for at home and traveling. They are the second-lightest material on our list. They are sturdier than material but less durable than wood or metal. They are easier to clean than most other types of crates and can double as a traveling crate if you choose an airline-approved crate.
- **wood:** Rigid, strong, and difficult to destroy. Wood crates tend to be favored for larger dog breeds. Their perks are

numerous. They can even double as furniture. These crates tend to be very heavy and bulky which means that when they've been set up, they are usually there forever. You might even need to do some assembly when you first get your crate. These crates are not as easy to clean as metal or plastic crates, but they are strong and safe.

- **metal:** Perhaps the most indestructible, metal crates are usually the preferred material for dog owners. They tend to be more mobile than wood crates, but more durable than any other type of crate. These are usually perfect for dogs that tend to chew other types of crates. While these crates might not be the best-looking crates, they can be beautified, and offer great ventilation for your pup.

Once you have chosen the correct crate for your pet, it's time to make sure that the crate is comfortable. The first step is to ensure that they can breathe. The crate should have enough ventilation to allow air in. Keep this in mind when purchasing the crate itself, but also when you purchase decorations and "furniture" for the crate. Speaking of furniture, your four-legged friend will need somewhere comfortable to sleep. This can usually be done by finding a dog bed. But you can even add some blankets to help keep the cold out and keep the floor more comfortable.

You can even add a few toys into your dog's crate to make them feel more at home. Lastly, you want to ensure that your dog always has a clean and full water bowl in their crate so that there is no danger of them becoming dehydrated.

DIY Crate Checklist

If you can't find the best crate for your furball and your home, or you just feel especially handy, you can always make your own crate out of wood. If this is a possibility for you, you can use this checklist to make sure you have everything you need.

Wood	
Nails/Screws	
Saw	
Drill	
Sandpaper	
Glue	
Hinges	
Latch/Lock	
Pet-safe paint/Sealant	
Padding	
Bedding	
Water Bowl	
Edge Protectors	

If you're more of a visual learner, you can find many tutorials on YouTube for how to create a crate for your dog. To help guide you in the right direction I have included a link to an easy-to-build, but extremely beautiful, functional, and perfect crate-

building video by the YouTube channel *Family Handyman* in the reference section.

SEVEN

Behavior Building Blocks

One of the major obstacles in pet ownership is the behavior of a pet. Will they be sweet and follow the rules, or will they be a terror like that family down the street whose dog is always barking, escaping, destroying everything, and doing whatever it takes to get their pictures added next to the word menace in the dictionary? Well, to overcome the obstacle of behavior, we first need to understand why these cute creatures often find themselves barking, chewing, biting, and embodying the naughty descriptor.

A Comprehensive Guide to Addressing Common Behavioral Issues

Four behavioral traits are generally seen as the difference between naughty and nice. These are chewing, biting, jumping on people, and jumping on furniture. We'll discuss each one now before we look at the solutions to these behaviors.

Chewing

We know that chewing is initially part of the teething process. We also know that we need to discourage this behavior. Yet, puppies are as crafty as they are cute. We often see puppies learn very quickly that if they chew something while there is a human nearby, they will get in trouble. So, instead of stopping their chewing, they simply start chewing when there is no human around to correct them.

If your puppy tends to chew a lot, there can be various reasons for this. One of the most common unnoticed reasons is that your puppy may have nutritional deficiencies. Yes, if their food is not giving them what they need, it can lead to chewing. However, their food might not be the only problem in the house. If your puppy seems to enjoy your carpet or furniture instead of other objects, there is a possibility that these objects may simply be tasty. In other words, someone may have spilled food, and these items still smell and taste good.

If your pup seems to be more interested in chewing walls or floors, you might want to look a bit deeper than the surface. Your pup might just be interested in getting behind the walls, or beneath the floors in search of other critters such as mice, raccoons, or other types of vermin and animals that could be hiding there.

Of course, there is also the possibility that your pet is simply bored out of their mind. If they do not receive enough interaction and have enough toys that they find interesting and enjoy

playing with, it could easily lead them to entertain themselves in more destructive ways.

The final reason for chewing is the most serious. Your pet might be engaging in what we call "escape behavior." This means that they do not feel comfortable in the space they are in and need to get away. But don't fret, it might not be your fault. There are a variety of reasons that your pet might be trying to get away, and this can include something as harmless as simply wanting to be with you.

Biting

When we're referring to biting in this section, we don't mean aggressively biting with the purpose of harming someone. This is more along the lines of biting while playing, which could lead to accidental harm. The problem with play-biting is that although it is not meant to be harmful or destructive, it can easily lead to broken skin, torn clothing, and in some cases, a full-on fight. Furthermore, biting is usually the precursor to growling and barking. Even in a playful sense. Once your puppy starts thinking this behavior is acceptable in a play sense, they will start to think it is acceptable in any sense.

The causes of this behavior can generally be traced back to human behavior. You see, this is usually an escalation of excitement that brings on the biting, which then further escalates to other forms of expression. So, be sure that when your pup is enjoying play time it is firstly not too rough, and the pup is in no way teased. The roughness encourages your pup to play rough as well, and since they cannot shove us like we would shove them,

they end up using their teeth. Being teased also encourages them to retaliate in the only way they know: with a snap of the jaw.

Of course, being confined for a long period of time will make anyone unhappy, including your pup. When you are unhappy with someone, how do you tend to convey these feelings? You tell them so. Which is exactly what your pup does when they are barking. This can, of course, then lead to biting again.

Lastly, excitement can also be a factor. When your pup sees a human who is excited, they will also become excited. Especially when this excitement is focused on your pup, such as when they are being greeted. Make sure that when your pup gets greeted, it does not happen with too much excitement.

Jumping on People

Jumping on people is something that either happens or doesn't. There is no "my dog sometimes jumps on people." This is behavior that is usually learned when puppies are small and cute, so everyone wants to pick them up. As they get bigger, people still want to pick them up, but seeing them use their little unstable legs is far too cute to resist. And that is where they start learning to put their paws on you.

This behavior is usually made worse and encouraged when your pets are greeted with intense energy. But this could also occur when your pet feels the need to get your attention, especially if they are starting to learn that they should not be using their voices.

Jumping on Furniture

Just like jumping on people, this behavior can easily be left over from their initial puppy experiences. When puppies are small and cute, they are generally sought after and enjoy the lap of luxury, quite literally. As they grow older, they want to continue laying on a lap like when they first met you, and since your lap is most often located on the furniture, they don't even need to wonder if they are allowed on there.

Of course, the furniture tends to be soft and comfortable. So, when your puppy finds themselves bored, these make easy targets for their teeth to be sunk into. Which brings us to the next point. Would you rather be comfortable while lying around getting into trouble, or would you be happy to do it on the cold, hard floors? The same goes for your puppy. Even if they are being naughty, they look for comfort, and if they cannot find enough soft spots on the floor, they will start to use your furniture as well.

Lastly, if an object that they desire is located on top of the couch, or the table next to the couch, your furry friend will see the couch as a stepping stone toward getting what they desire. After all, you usually put your butt on it, so why can't they put their paws on there?

Practical Solutions and Examples to Correct These Behaviors

As you can see, most of the so-called naughty behavior that a pet tends to exhibit can either be directly correlated to human behavior, or to your pet not being stimulated enough. We've

already identified the human behavior that could lead to this naughty behavior, and the answer to them is simple. Make sure that you and anyone else your pet interacts with are conscious about how you interact with your pet from day one and do not teach them behavior that is unacceptable.

While engaging in training with your pet will already help a great deal with mental stimulation, there are still some pups out there who seem to sleep next to a nuclear power station every night, and then still wake up by chugging down a couple of gallons of clean caffeine. These pups might need some extra stimulation. So here are a few ideas of how you can stimulate your pup.

Play Games

Games like hide-and-seek and finding objects help to stimulate your dog, not only by letting them get rid of their energy, and think of where you are, but they also get to use some of their other abilities such as their extremely sensitive sense of smell. By letting your pup find you, you can help them to appropriately release their emotions so that they are calmer in other situations. While finding objects such as their toys or treats reward them for using their energy at appropriate times.

Walks

A walk allows your dog to get out of the house and experience new scenery and new smells while meeting new people and other dogs. These next experiences are great for stimulating your pup, but they can be taken to the next level quite easily.

One of the ways of making walks more interesting is by making them scent walks. These are walks during which you focus more on letting your dog explore smells and follow the journey their nose comes up with at their own time than walking a specific distance. Did you know that allowing your dog to use their noses a bit actually lowers their heart rate and causes their brain to release the chemicals that make them feel happy?

Additionally, you can also mix up the routes you take for your walk and try to always find new routes. By taking a new route you expose your pet to even more new environments and stimulants without having to go too far out of the way. Think of it in this way, when you repeat the same routine day after day, after day, after day you get just as bored with it, as you would have gotten if I said "after day" one more time. The same goes for your dog. Repetition can lead to boredom.

Spice Up Their Everyday.

You might not always be there to play games with your pet, or to take them exploring. So, you need to look into ways you can change their everyday lives. One of these is giving them puzzles and interactive toys that they can keep themselves busy with while you are not there. Puzzles and interactive toys usually hide food in a manner that forces your dog to work a bit harder before they can get their reward, and yes, they do have the capacity to come up with ideas on how to get their treats, and many dogs tend to enjoy this activity.

If your dog does find it a bit difficult to figure out their toys or puzzles, or they simply don't have the patience for it, you can try frozen treats. I recently saw a video on social media where a pet owner froze some fruit in water, in such a way that it created an ice bowl. He would then fill the bowl with water and put it out on extremely hot days. This gave his dog a nice cool and fresh bowl of water on a day when they really needed it, while also giving the dog a treat to work to that kept them engaged and cool for an extended period of time during the day. You can also give your pet a frozen treat when you leave for work or on an errand as a way to keep them calm and engaged for the first few hours after you leave, this can help them to accept having to separate from you.

Another way to use their food to stimulate them is a technique called scatter feeding. At mealtime, you keep your dog in a certain area while you take their food and place them in small piles all around the house. This means that your dog does need to put a bit of effort into finding their food, but not so much that they need to think too hard about it or feel like they are not being fed properly.

Finally, constantly introducing new toys into their lives is also an amazing way to keep them stimulated. Just like children, they tend to get bored with the same things over and over, and this unfortunately does extend to their toys as well. By regularly changing out old toys and bringing in new toys you ensure that your pet does not get bored with their old toys.

Advice on How to Prevent Future Behavioral Problems From Arising

While you should by now be competent in correcting bad behavior and training your dog on how to act appropriately, there are still ways to ensure that you do not accidentally encourage more bad behavior in the future, and prevention is always preferred to correction.

- Keep your commands consistent. Don't change the verbal cue or the hand signal after some time has passed, as this will basically reset your pup's training back to the beginning.
- Ensure that bad behavior is not met with any type of attention at all. We tend to want to console our pets after they engage in bad behavior, especially if this behavior ends badly for them, but this can be seen as a reward that will end up encouraging the behavior.
- Ensure that good behavior is regularly rewarded. Remember this is the basis of our positive reinforcement techniques.
- Exercise is one of the best ways to help your puppy get rid of any pent-up energy that can lead them into temptation, this is also a great opportunity to refresh their training.
- Ask for advice, whether from professionals or in your training communities. Of course, advice from non-professionals needs to be researched and checked before implementation, but others who have working knowledge on training dogs can have valuable insight

into helping you ensure that bad behavior is discouraged before it is allowed to take root.

Behavioral Issue Tracker

Just as how we want to track the positive reinforcement and reward, we use with our pets, it is important to track their bad behavior as well. By tracking bad behavior, you become aware when new behavior arises, when you manage to effectively discourage poor behavior, and if this behavior starts to become worse.

This tracker works almost exactly the same as the positive reinforcement tracker and can be filled in the same way.

Date	Time	Behavior Observed	Situation in Which Behavior Occurred	How Was the Behavior Handled?

EIGHT

Family Fido

Having a puppy is amazing, but having a puppy join your family can be extremely chaotic. You might have certain rules, or discourage certain behavior, that your partner might not agree with or find endearing. While your partner or even other family members might not be actively trying to go against your wishes, they could still end up encouraging behaviors that you have deemed a no-no without realizing it. This is why it is crucial that the entire family be involved in the training of the newest family member.

The Importance of Involving Children and Other Family Members in the Puppy Training Process

Unlike humans, dogs are literally born to be in big families. When a dog gives birth, they usually give birth to an entire litter, whereas humans generally only give birth to one child at a time. This means that pups are born with a deeper sense of family

dynamics than we are and rely on them more than we do. So, they need to not only understand where they fit into your "pack" but also where you fit into it.

This is not the only reason that your family needs to be involved. That bond and level of communication we've discussed a few times now is something that can only be found during training. When you teach your pet how to communicate with you, they are also learning how you communicate with people in general. So, when other family members try to communicate with them and you two don't speak the same language, this can become a problem. For example, you are teaching your furry friend that when you give them a command, they only get rewarded if they obey it immediately. But another family member might come along and repeat the command several times, without waiting for your pet to actually obey it. Your pet won't understand why the language is suddenly changed, and something new is expected from them. So, they might not be sure whether they should listen to your language or the other person's language, especially if they are unsure who is the leader of their strange pack.

Kids And Pups

Depending on the age of your child, they might need to learn along with your newest family member. Kids often see puppies as very animated toys that they can play with in the same manner that they play with their other toys. By having your kids partici-pate in the training sessions, you have the opportunity to show them that the puppy is, in fact, not a toy, but a living and

breathing animal that has emotions, thoughts, and most impor-
tantly, can feel pain, annoyance, and love.

This also gives your kid the opportunity to learn what the right
way is to not only play with but to generally interact with the
family pet. If I had a penny for each time I've seen kids get hurt
because they didn't know that pulling a puppy by its tail is
wrong, I could probably retire quite comfortably. Of course,
teaching them the right way is not only about how to interact
with your pup but also how to communicate in the same way you
do to ensure that there is no confusion for your pup on how to
take commands or whom to listen to.

This also gives you the perfect opportunity to teach your child
how to read the body language of your pup. This is an extremely
handy ability for your children to have. They will be able to identify when they are annoying your pup, and when there is something or someone in the area that they feel threatened by and
they can learn when the pup needs to go outside, or into their
crate for some well-deserved me-time.

Finally, having your kid engaged in training with your pup also
encourages the bond between the two of them to grow stronger.
This means that your child will also have a positive and happy
experience with the new puppy, and they can also enjoy the pure,
unrestricted love of a dog.

Tips for Getting Everyone on the Same Page and Ensuring
Consistency in Training

As we've established by now, everyone in your family needs to be on the same page about where your pup is in their training, what is expected of them, and how to get this from them. Your family should also remain consistent in the training technique used for your pup, how they communicate with the pup, and what behavior is allowed. This is no easy feat, especially when there are children involved. So here are some tips to help you with this.

- Be clear about what you expect from your family. Each family member needs to know exactly what you need them to do, and what you need them not to do.
- Boundaries need to be placed. No, you cannot allow the pup to sleep on your bed. No, you cannot get in the crate with the pup. Yes, the pup may have two treats per day when they obey commands. These are basic rules that should be kept in place and followed by everyone.
- Be careful with your way of communicating with your family. They understand you better than your puppy, but chances are they will also respond better to positive reinforcements and patience. Avoid using accusations, and generalizations. Instead of saying "You always let the pup get on the couch, you are messing with their training," try saying; "I feel like the pup gets away with breaking rules when they are with you, and I've noticed this translates into them ignoring other aspects of their training, would you be willing to..."

- Accept it when your family says no. You cannot control their behavior. So, when they say no, look for a different solution together that both parties can agree on.
- Keep others informed of your training requirements. You can place a sign near where you are training to inform others what you require during your training sessions, or you can even create information leaflets that can be given to anyone who needs to enter the training environment.
- Regularly re-evaluate your training approach. Especially when something goes wrong. This allows you to understand when you need to take a different approach yourself, get advice or insights from your family, or encourage them to change their approach.
- Be aware of your own emotions. When you feel a period of heightened emotions, it's generally a good idea to not partake in training or discuss aspects of training with your family. Wait until your emotions have calmed down and you are able to have a logical conversation with your family instead of an emotional one.
- Forgive easily. Your family is also trying to show your pup love and affection in their own way. They are also human, and mistakes will be made. But we need to keep the training a positive and happy experience for everyone, so don't dwell on mistakes. Remember when your family feels negative about training, your pup will pick up on this.
- Keep an eye on the emotions of others. While you are not responsible for their emotions, you need to keep the training session as emotion-free as you can. If you see a family member who is involved in training having

negative emotions, it might be best to stop the training immediately and pick back up once that family member has calmed down a bit. (Please don't tell them to calm down, we all know how well that works!)

- Hold regular family meetings during which time your family is allowed to communicate their feelings and opinions without fear of being shut down, or facing consequences for not agreeing with you, or for admitting to mistakes. Honesty is the best policy, and your family needs to be able to honestly discuss the training to ensure that everyone stays on the same page.

Training with your family can be extremely difficult. But once everyone is on the same page, it can be tenfold more rewarding. Your pup's training can even become a family bonding experience that will not only strengthen the bond with the puppy but also between the humans.

Real-Life Examples of Families Successfully Training Their Puppy Together

My friend Matt had another story for me that I felt would fit in here quite well. You see the company he worked for had been approached by a dog-dad in the community they are situated in.

The man that approached them had an American Bulldog puppy of about nine months old named Bella. He also had two daughters aged six and seven. These two girls absolutely adored Bella. Bella on the other hand barely tolerated these two girls, and she outright hated anyone else. The dad found himself in a difficult

position. He either had to get Bella to behave, surrender her to a rescue organization, or send her to the farm up north. While she had never bitten the girls, she had come close on a few occasions, and she had bitten several humans already. It was only a miracle that Animal Control had not yet gotten involved.

Matt's company agreed to help train Bella and get her through this difficult time. Bella's dad had been a bit scared of keeping Bella at home until she was fully trained based on an incident with his girls that occurred the previous night. You see, Bella hated water more than she hated humans, and the girls had gone for a swim. This angered Bella.

It didn't take the professional trainers at Matt's work long to establish that Bella survived a bad run-in with the pool shortly after she had come home. The trainers were also not too surprised to hear that this run-in was caused by the family's gardener who, out of fear of dogs, had abused Bella for months when the family would leave the home before eventually being caught and fired.

Unfortunately, the damage was done. While the trainers would have preferred Bella to stay home, they understood why her dad wanted her to be boarded at the company while she received her training.

The first challenge that the trainers had to face was to get Bella into a kennel. It was a confined space she did not feel safe in, and she hated a collar around her neck. Of course, nobody was brave enough to pick her up and carry her into the kennel either. It took several hours of Bella's dad calming her down with treats in the back of his pick-up and playing nice before he managed to

coax a collar and leash around her neck and move her toward the kennel. The moment she was in the kennel, Bella was once again aggressive and tried to chew through the metal in search of a victim for her teeth.

Over the next three months, Matt's manager and the family worked together with Bella. At first, the family would come in and sit outside the kennel while Bella ferociously made her emotions regarding their betrayal clear. Whenever she would stop barking and biting toward them, they would give her a treat. Of course, this treat had to be thrown through the side of the kennel, but it was a start.

When Bella finally allowed them to sit next to the Kennel for a day without becoming aggressive, the next part of the training was implemented. Getting her to allow them to touch her. Dad was first; he held a treat in his hand near the side of the kennel and allowed Bella to sniff. This gave her his scent, along with the scent of the treat. Then the treat was brought as close as possible before being dropped into the kennel. This repetition continued until Dad could give the treat without Bella trying to bite his fingers as well.

From here on, Dad would place his palm against the side of the kennel, and when Bella rubbed or laid, or in any way interacted with the hand in a non-violent way, she would quickly enjoy a treat. This continued with slow and minor escalations until Dad was able to reach his hand into the kennel and touch Bella all over her body without any danger.

During the time that Bella was being reintroduced to her dad, she was also introduced to Matt's manager who would be running the training. First, Dad would reach a successful milestone, and then the manager would follow.

Eventually, Bella allowed her dad to place a collar around her neck, and at first, she just sat with it in her kennel. After a few sessions like this, Dad was to take Bella out of her kennel on the leash. This is when the first setback occurred. You see, up until this point whenever Bella was let out of her kennel, she had done so with as little human interaction as possible, to ensure that the time she spent outside her kennel was positive, and that she could relieve herself, get some exercise, and not build up stress, while her kennel was being cleaned as well. This was the first time in almost two weeks that she was outside her kennel with a human within biting distance. She went for it. Luckily everyone was prepared for this exact event, and she didn't hurt Dad in any way. Her training took a few steps backward and she slowly regained her trust in Dad.

Eventually, she was brought out again, and this time it went so much better. The training continued to escalate until Dad could coax Bella into the designated training enclosure. Here Bella was at first released with the collar and leash still around her neck. She immediately took off and spent most of her time on the opposite side of the enclosure from where Dad and the manager were, but she did not show them any type of aggression until they had to take her back to the kennel. This time, however, she only growled a bit and resisted their movements towards the kennel. With some treats and a lot of patience, this problem too was overcome.

By week three Bella was ready to start being introduced to the girls again. Once again it started off slowly, but this time instead of introducing Bella to them in her kennel, she was being introduced in the training area. In fact, the training enclosure had become the "communal space" where Bella showed the least amount of aggression. Her Kennel had once again become her own space where nobody entered aside from her Dad, or the trainer when they brought her food or fetched her to go to the communal space.

The introduction with the girls went a lot smoother and faster than the introduction with the dad. Her tolerance of them, and understanding of communal space, meant that there was very little aggression. Once Bella got to know the daughters again, and they too could both enter the enclosure and touch Bella without much problem, it was time for some more training. As usual, they started with the sit command. There was the second major setback.

The first time Bella realized that she did not have total freedom and that something was expected from her that she might not have particularly wanted to do out of her own free will, the old Bella resurfaced. It was only at week five that Bella sat down for the first time. Once she did, however, it was as if a switch had flipped inside her brain. By week six, the girls were attending training with Dad, and Bella started to show real changes in her demeanor and attitude toward people.

By week 11, the six-year-old could put a collar around Bella's neck, attach the leash, and take this puppy for a walk. Bella was now 14 months old, but she had grown to be the perfect family

pet, and her family once again trusted Bella completely. They trusted her so much that they took her home, armed with a plan that was approved by the manager on how to train Bella to accept the pool. In fact, Bella surprised everyone the day she placed her first tentative paw into the swimming pool.

It was almost a year after her training had started. Her family had managed to slowly get her used to the idea that the family would spend time in the swimming pool, and that this was in no way a danger to her. Over time, Bella started coming closer and closer to the pool. The family never thought she would go any further than the edge, but after she saw the fun her two favorite girls were having in the pool, she decided to work on her fear on her own. As everyone ran into the pool one hot summer day, Bella ran up to the side of the pool, stopped dead in her tracks, gave the family a bark to get their attention, and sniffed the water before placing a paw in it. She quickly retracted the paw, twirled in a circle a few times, and then went on with her day. Over the coming months, she would take her face closer to the water, and keep placing her paw deeper and deeper, until she somehow worked through her own trauma and worked her way into the pool on her own.

When last Matt heard from the family, Bella was still somewhat careful, but she actually sat on the top step of the pool and watched the family swim. Bella is the perfect example of how much progress and change can be made when a family trains together, under the leadership of a professional.

Family Training Plan

To help you and your family I've created a family plan to ensure that everyone has a place in this journey. For each role you can fill in the family member's name, the form already has their requirements in, you can add in what you expect them to accomplish and add in a schedule for when they are supposed to interact with the pup in their capacity.

Name	Role	Training Requirements	Expectations	Schedule
	Primary Trainer	Teach Basic commands and determining cues.		
	Secondary Trainer	Use commands and cues as determined by Primary.		
	Supervision	Avoid discipline or corrective actions, and focus on redirecting attention instead.		

Now that you've unlocked the secrets to puppy training, it's time to share the love and guide fellow puppy enthusiasts on their training journey. Your newfound knowledge is a valuable asset, and by leaving your honest opinion of "Puppy Training Made Easy: A Step-By-Step Guide to Prep Your Home, Teach Basic Commands, and Create a Lifelong Bond with Dogs of All Personalities" on Amazon, you're playing a crucial role in passing the leash to others.

Simply by sharing your thoughts, you'll help other puppy owners:

...discover the paw-sitive impact of The Puppy Prodigy Method.

...navigate the challenges of puppyhood with confidence.

...create a bond with their furry friends that lasts a lifetime.

Thank you for being a vital part of this journey. Puppy owner-ship thrives when we pass on our knowledge, and you're helping us do just that.

Scan the QR code to leave your review!

Your review is a beacon of guidance for those seeking puppy wisdom. Together, let's create a community where every furry friend finds a loving home and every owner discovers the joy of a well-trained companion.

Thank you for your paw-some contribution!

Conclusion

We've finally reached the conclusion of our time together. You are now fully equipped to welcome a new puppy into your home and help them not only fit in with your family but become part of your family.

We've covered quite a lot of ground in this book, and I want you to take a moment and look back on the journey you and your pup have no doubt had throughout these pages. You have learned how to carefully prepare your home to suit your pups needs and ensure your pup is welcomed into your family with open arms.

You've managed to start their training from day one, and while I have no doubt that there were some hiccups along the way, I am equally certain that you and your pup both used these as learning opportunities. I can only imagine the excitement you both shared with each other the first time your pup realized that when you say sit, they should lower their bums to get a treat. And to see that simple first steps evolve into a well-behaved pup that looks

at you and your family with love and adoration is one of the best feelings in the world.

We've covered the benefits of positive reinforcement and looked at the different techniques available to you. From clicking and treats to affection and toys, whichever reward you choose to use on your pup will certainly help to develop their personality and grow the bond between the two of you even more.

When your pup is in their crate, I am sure they are dreaming of the next reward they get from you, and wondering how the universe decided that they should be lucky enough to find a home with an amazing pack like the one living in your "den."

While our journey must unfortunately end, the journey with your pup has just begun. If pups like Bella, Jack, and all the others we couldn't include in our pages can find happy endings to their story, your pup's happy life is more than assured.

As we take our leave from each other I would like to ask you to give this book a review, share how it helped you, and recommend it where you can. Not only do I enjoy hearing the stories of how families become stronger when a well-trained pup joins the pack, but your review might also just help someone with their own Jack or Bella to find this book, and in doing so you will help another pup and their family to find a happy ending to their story.

My wish for you and your furry friend is a long life filled with unconditional love and fierce loyalty. And a special woof for all the pups that make our journey through life so much better, by just being with us.

References

The art of positive dog training: building a strong bond. (2023, September 6). The Grand Paw. https://thegrandpaw.com/the-art-of-positive-dog-training-building-a-strong-bond/

The benefits of crate training. (n.d.). PAWS. https://www.paws.org/resources/the-benefits-of-crate-training/

The benefits of puppies for kids! (2020, August 31). The Puppy Academy. https://www.thepuppyacademy.com/blog/2020/8/31/the-benefits-of-puppies-for-kids

The benefits of using a dog harness: A guide for dog owners. (2023, July 24). K9 Active. https://www.k9active.co.uk/blog/the-benefits-of-using-a-dog-harness-a-guide-for-dog-owners

The benefits of using a dog playpen for your puppy. (2023, June 2). Off Leash Blog; Fi. https://blog.tryfi.com/is-dog-playpen-good-for-puppies/

The best fetch toy for dogs. (n.d.). Preventive Vet. https://www.preventivevet.com/the-best-fetch-toy-for-dogs

Anderson, O. (2019). *All aboard: Why getting the whole family involved in training will help Fido learn.* How I Met My Dog. https://www.howimetmydog.com/index.php/blog/all-aboard-why-getting-the-whole-family-involved-in-training-will-help-fido-learn

Andre, J. (2020, August 3). *Why keeping a dog journal is valuable and rewarding.* SohoSpark. https://sohospark.com/blogs/news/how-to-keep-a-dog-journal

April, J. P. (2021, July 15). *5 Basic commands to teach your new puppy.* Furtropolis. https://outwardhound.com/furtropolis/dogs/5-basic-commands-to-teach-your-new-puppy

Are you a good dog trainer? (2017, June 16). Quizony. https://www.quizony.com/are-you-a-good-dog-trainer/index.html

Arford, K. (2019, November 19). *crate training benefits: why a crate is great for you and your dog.* American Kennel Club. https://www.akc.org/expert-advice/training/why-crate-training-is-great-for-your-dog/

Arford, K. (2020, October 20). *10 Science-based benefits of having a dog.* American Kennel Club. https://www.akc.org/expert-advice/lifestyle/10-science-based-benefits-dog/

Avis-Riordan, K. (2018, March 8). *9 top tips on how to train your puppy from day one, according to an expert dog trainer*. Country Living. https://www.countryliving. com/uk/wildlife/pets/advice/a3459/how-to-train-puppy-dogs-trust-train ing-expert/

Basics of clicker training. (2020, February 19). BatterSea. https://www.battersea. org.uk/pet-advice/dog-advice/basics-clicker-training

Becker, M. (2022, September 14). *7 Tips for training a stubborn dog*. Vetstreet. https://www.vetstreet.com/our-pet-experts/7-strategies-for-training-a-stub born-dog

Bowen, J. (2022, June 22). *How to prevent behavior problems in puppies*. Vet Focus. https://vetfocus.royalcanin.com/en/scientific/how-to-prevent-behavior-prob lems-in-puppies

Bowen, J., & Heath, S. (2005). *Clicker training - an overview*. Science Direct. https:// www.sciencedirect.com/topics/agricultural-and-biological-sciences/clicker-training

Building a relationship with positive reinforcement. (n.d.). Our Companions Animal Rescue. https://www.ourcompanions.org/dogs/dog-behavior-services/build ing-a-relationship-with-positive-reinforcement/

Burton, B. (2021). *Does clicker training lead to faster acquisition of behavior for dog owners? It depends on the behavior*. The IAABC Foundation. https://journal.iaabc foundation.org/does-clicker-training-lead-to-faster-acquisition-of-behavior-for-dog-owners-it-depends-on-the-behavior/

C, V. (n.d.). *Top 7 reasons to crate train your dog*. Now Fresh. https://nowfresh.com/ en-us/top-reasons-to-crate-train-your-dog

Caroline. (2022, April 8). *The impact of patience in dog training and rehabilitation*. Gooddoggie. https://www.gooddoggie.co.uk/learning-patience-for-dog-train ing-and-rehabilitation/

Case, L. P. (2017, April 24). *Why we click*. The Science Dog. https://thesciencedog. com/2017/04/24/why-we-click/

Chopik, W. J., & Weaver, J. R. (2019). Old dog, new tricks: Age differences in dog personality traits, associations with human personality traits, and links to important outcomes. *Journal of Research in Personality, 79*, 94–108. https://doi. org/10.1016/j.jrp.2019.01.005

Clicker training. (n.d.). Gun Dog Forum. http://gundogforum.com/forum/view topic.php?t=51474

Clicker training your dog. (n.d.). PDSA. https://www.pdsa.org.uk/pet-help-and-advice/looking-after-your-pet/puppies-dogs/clicker-training

Coes, J. (2018, July 16). *Top 4 challenges new puppy owners face.* Peaceful Paws Pet Care. https://peacefulpawspetcare.com/2018/07/16/top-4-challenges-new-puppy-owners-face/

Collins, A. (2023, January 20). *Tips and tricks for tiring out your high energy pup.* Atlas Pet Company. https://atlaspetcompany.com/blogs/adventures/tips-tricks-tiring-out-your-high-energy-pup

Common dog behavior issues. (2015). ASPCA. https://www.aspca.org/pet-care/dog-care/common-dog-behavior-issues

Common puppy training mistakes new owners make! (2020, January 6). The Puppy Academy. https://www.thepuppyacademy.com/blog/2020/1/6/common-puppy-training-mistakes-new-owners-make

Complete guide to bringing home a new puppy (with checklists) (2021, February 5). Jet Pet Resort. https://jetpetresort.com/blog/dog-care/guide-bringing-home-new-puppy-checklists/

Complete puppy training schedule by age! (n.d.). The Puppy Academy. Retrieved December 18, 2023, from https://www.thepuppyacademy.com/blog/2020/8/24/complete-puppy-training-schedule-by-age

Coren, S. (2010, December 28). *Reward training vs. discipline-based dog training Psychology Today.* Www.psychologytoday.com. https://www.psychologytoday.com/us/blog/canine-corner/201012/reward-training-vs-discipline-based-dog-training

Correcting dog behavior: How to stop bad dog behavior. (2021, January 11). American Kennel Club. https://www.akc.org/expert-advice/training/how-to-curb-unwanted-dog-behaviors/

Crate rest: Bedding. (2017, March 27). The Rehab Vet. https://therehabvet.com/2017/03/bedding-during-crate-rest/

Crate training 101. (2018). The Humane Society of the United States. https://www.humanesociety.org/resources/crate-training-101

Dangerous toys and chews for puppies. (2023, August 15). Pupford. https://pupford.com/dangerous-toys-chews-puppies/

Day, L. (2019, May 15). *Crate training a puppy while at work – A four-step guide.* Www.pupbox.com. https://www.pupbox.com/training/crate-training-a-puppy-while-at-work/

Developmental stages of puppy behavior. (n.d.). PAWS. Retrieved December 5, 2023, from https://www.paws.org/resources/developmental-stages-of-puppy-behavior/

Different dog personalities and how to best train them. (2020, October 31). Pets in

Omaha. https://petsinomaha.com/different-dog-personalities-and-how-to-best-train-them/

Does clicker training for dogs really work? (2017, August 24). The Shot Spot. https://theshotspot.org/news/does-clicker-training-work-for-dogs/

Dog training clickers: advice & information. (n.d.). My Pet and I. https://mypetandi.elanco.com/en_gb/pet-training-tips-and-tricks/when-dog-training-just-clicks-everything-you-need-know-about-dog

Dog training commands: Consistent dog training. (2018, August 10). American Kennel Club. https://www.akc.org/expert-advice/training/importance-consistency-training-dog/

Dogs often take on the same personality traits as their owner. (2023, June 1). Farmer Pete's. https://www.farmerpetes.com.au/blogs/blog/dogs-same-personality-traits-as-owner

Donovan, L. (2019, October 31). *Puppy socialization: how to socialize a puppy.* American Kennel Club. https://www.akc.org/expert-advice/training/puppy-socialization/

8 Ways to make training sessions with your dog more fun. (2023, October 20). Pupford.com. https://pupford.com/make-dog-training-sessions-fun/

Erb, H. (2018, January 22). *Give it time! When it comes to dog training, Patience is important.* American Kennel Club. https://www.akc.org/expert-advice/training/dog-training-patience-important/

Erickson, J. (2018, May 9). *Dog care chore chart for children (by age)» The Stay-at-Home-Mom Survival Guide.* The Stay-At-Home-Mom Survival Guide. https://thestay-at-home-momsurvivalguide.com/dog-care-chore-chart-children-by-age/

Esposito, D. (2021, May 21). *How to teach your new dog 7 basic cues.* The Dodo. https://www.thedodo.com/dodowell/basic-dog-commands

Feng, L. C., Howell, T. J., & Bennett, P. C. (2016). How clicker training works: Comparing Reinforcing, Marking, and Bridging Hypotheses. *Applied Animal Behaviour Science, 181,* 34–40. https://doi.org/10.1016/j.applanim.2016.05.012

Feyrecilde, M., Horwitz, D., & Landsberg, G. (2009). *Puppy behavior and training - Training basics.* VCA Animal Hospitals. https://vcahospitals.com/know-your-pet/puppy-behavior-and-training-training-basics

5 Benefits of clicker training. (2022, March 11). Thousand Hills Pets Resort. https://www.thousandhillspetresort.com/post/5-benefits-of-clicker-training

Fratt, K. (2023, March 19). *Reward-based training versus punishment: Which is better?*

/ *Journey Dog Training*. Journeydogtraining.com. https://journeydogtraining. com/reward-based-training-versus-punishment-which-is-better/

Geier, E. (n.d.). *Quiz: What's your dog's personality archetype?* The Dog People. https://www.rover.com/blog/quiz-whats-dogs-personality-archetype/

Geller, T. (2005, December 28). *Got a new puppy? Advice on how to adjust.* Today. https://www.today.com/news/got-new-puppy-advice-how-adjust-wbna10628490

Gibeault, S. (2018, April 30). *Positive rewards dog training tips.* American Kennel Club. https://www.akc.org/expert-advice/training/training-rewards/

Gibeault, S. (2019, December 24). *Clicker training: learn about mark & reward dog training using clickers.* American Kennel Club. https://www.akc.org/expert-advice/training/clicker-training-your-dog-mark-and-reward/

Gibeault, S. (2021a, April 20). *Puppy exercise & activities for training your puppy.* American Kennel Club. https://www.akc.org/expert-advice/training/keep-your-puppy-active-and-out-of-trouble-with-stimulation-and-exercise/

Gibeault, S. (2021b, June 16). *positive reinforcement dog training: the science behind operant conditioning.* American Kennel Club. https://www.akc.org/expert-advice/training/operant-conditioning-the-science-behind-positive-reinforce ment-dog-training/

Goodnight, K. (n.d.). *The benefits of training your puppy.* 24Petwatch. https://www. 24petwatch.com/blog/the-benefits-of-training-your-puppy

Grenus, B. (2023, May 18). *9 Cost-effective ways to keep your dog mentally stimulated.* PetMD. https://www.petmd.com/dog/general-health/ways-to-keep-dog-mentally-stimulated

Hartstein, R. (2014, December 9). *Dog training and family participation* Fun Paw Care. https://www.funpawcare.com/2014/12/09/dog-training-and-family-participation/

Hecht, J. (2022, December 13). *Does your dog have a personality?* The Wildest. https://www.thewildest.com/dog-behavior/dogs-personalities

Heimbuch, J. (2022, December 19). *The 6 biggest challenges all new puppy owners face.* Treehugger. https://www.treehugger.com/the-biggest-challenges-all-new-puppy-owners-face-4863781

Help your anxious or fearful dog gain confidence. (n.d.). Animal Humane Society. https://www.animalhumanesociety.org/resource/help-your-anxious-or-fear ful-dog-gain-confidence

Horwitz, D., & Landsberg, G. (n.d.). *Using reinforcement and rewards to train your*

pet. VCA Animal Hospitals. https://vcahospitals.com/know-your-pet/using-reinforcement-and-rewards-to-train-your-pet

Household Harmony: Introducing a second dog to your home. (2012, August 13). Cold Nose Companions. https://www.coldnosecompanions.com/household-harmony-introducing-a-second-dog-to-your-home/

How do you train a dog to stop destructive chewing? (2018, May 24). Www.petassure.com. https://www.petassure.com/new-newsletters/how-do-you-train-a-dog-to-stop-destructive-chewing/

How to build a DIY dog crate. (2023). [YouTube Tutorial]. In *Family Handyman*. https://www.youtube.com/watch?v=vTXhaBFSZGc

How to clicker train your dog: 7-step training guide. (2021, June 7). Master Class. https://www.masterclass.com/articles/how-to-clicker-train-your-dog

How to establish a routine and boundaries with your puppy. (2016, August 9). American Kennel Club. https://www.akc.org/expert-advice/training/how-to-establish-a-routine-and-boundaries-with-your-puppy/

How to help your new puppy adjust to your home. (2019, January 11). Dogtopia. https://www.dogtopia.com/blog/new-puppy-adjust-to-house/

How to house train and crate train a puppy. (n.d.). Small Door Veterinary. Retrieved December 22, 2023, from https://www.smalldoorvet.com/learning-center/puppies-kittens/housetraining-and-crate-training

How to introduce A new puppy? (2018, October 3). Royal Canin. https://www.royalcanin.com/us/dogs/puppy/introducing-your-puppy-to-family-members

How to keep a pet journal! Create a journal for your cat or dog! (2022, August 9) WashiGang. https://www.washigang.com/blogs/news/how-to-keep-a-pet-journal

How to reward your dog and a List of reinforcements (2023, November 7). Pupford.com. https://pupford.com/reward-your-dog-and-reinforcements/

How to stop puppy biting. (2023, November 9). American Kennel Club. https://www.akc.org/expert-advice/training/stop-puppy-biting/

How to train a timid dog: 13 steps. (n.d.). WikiHow. Retrieved December 7, 2023, from https://www.wikihow.com/Train-a-Timid-Dog

How to use a clicker for dog training: Tips & tricks. (2021, September 24). The Dog Wizard. https://thedogwizard.com/blog/how-to-use-a-clicker-for-dog-training/

The Humane Society of The United States. (n.d.). *Positive reinforcement training*. The Humane Society of the United States. Retrieved December 22, 2023, from https://www.humanesociety.org/resources/positive-reinforcement-training

The importance of consistency in dog training. (2022, May 20). Gooddoggie. https://www.gooddoggie.co.uk/consistency-in-dog-training/

Introducing your new dog to your other dogs. (n.d.). The Humane Society of the United States. Retrieved December 9, 2023, from https://www.humanesociety.org/resources/introducing-new-dogs

Jones, S. (2013, April 24). *Aggressive dog training tips: Calming the beast.* CanineJournal.com. https://www.caninejournal.com/aggressive-dog-training-tips/

Jumping, chewing, playbiting, and other destructive behavior problems in puppies, Young Dogs. (2010, May 29). PetMD. https://www.petmd.com/dog/conditions/behavioral/c_dg_pediatric_behavior_problems

Kellar, J. (2022, March 16). *Getting your new pet settled at home.* Houston SPCA. https://houstonspca.org/easy-ways-to-strengthen-the-bond-with-your-pet/

Kim. (2013, March 19). *What you should and should NOT do with the clicker.* Training Canines. https://trainingcanines.com/what-you-should-and-should-not-do-with-the-clicker/

Lessa, E. (2023, June 20). *How to train a dog with positive reinforcement.* PetMD. https://www.petmd.com/dog/behavior/how-to-train-a-dog-with-positive-reinforcement

Lindell, E., Feyrecilde, M., Horwitz, D., & Landsberg, G. (n.d.). *Puppy behavior and training - Socialization and fear prevention.* VCA Animal Hospitals. https://vcahospitals.com/know-your-pet/puppy-behavior-and-training---socialization-and-fear-prevention

London, K. B. (2020, November 11). *Here are 9 common dog-training mistakes.* The Wildest. https://www.thewildest.com/dog-behavior/common-dog-training-mistakes

Lunchick, P. (2018, September 25). *Teach your puppy these 5 basic commands.* American Kennel Club. https://www.akc.org/expert-advice/training/teach-your-puppy-these-5-basic-commands/

M., H. (n.d.). *Clicker training for puppies.* ASPCA. Retrieved December 22, 2023, from https://www.aspcapetinsurance.com/resources/clicker-training-puppies/

Madaus, J. (2021, August 20). *Essential items for a new puppy. Water bowl and food bowl.* Bubi Bottle. https://bubibottle.com/essential-items-for-a-new-puppy-water-bowl-and-food-bowl/

Madson, C. (2019a, February 10). *How to set up a long–term puppy confinement area.* Preventive Vet. https://www.preventivevet.com/dogs/how-to-set-up-puppy-

long-term-confinement-area

Madson, C. (2019b, February 10). *How to set up a safe space for your dog.* Preventive Vet. https://www.preventivevet.com/dogs/how-to-set-up-a-safe-space-for-your-dog

Madson, C. (2020a, March 10). *How to use toys as rewards in dog training.* Preventive Vet. https://www.preventivevet.com/dogs/toy-rewards-in-dog-training

Madson, C. (2020b, June 6). Dog *trainer tips: Puppy nipping and biting* Www.preventivevet.com. https://www.preventivevet.com/dogs/puppy-nipping-and-biting

Martin, K. M. (2017). World Small Animal Veterinary Association Congress Proceedings, 2017. *VIN.com.* https://www.vin.com/apputil/content/default adv1.aspx?id=8506439&pId=20539

Martin, N. (2023, October 2). *The new puppy checklist: Essentials for pet parents.* Rover; The Dog People. https://www.rover.com/blog/reviews/new-puppy-checklist/

McCafferty, C. (2017). *Top 5 clicker training mistakes.* Petlife. https://vocal.media/petlife/top-5-clicker-training-mistakes

Mental & physical Stimulation: Is your dog getting what they need? (2019, December 31). Petcetera Animal Clinic. https://www.petcgfk.com/mental-physical-stimulation-is-your-dog-getting-what-they-need/

Meyers, H. (2019, August 9). *Puppy-proofing tips for your home and yard.* American Kennel Club. https://www.akc.org/expert-advice/puppy-information/puppy-proofing-tips-for-your-home-and-yard/

Mouthing, nipping and biting in puppies. (n.d.). ASPCA. https://www.aspca.org/pet-care/dog-care/common-dog-behavior-issues/mouthing-nipping-and-biting-puppies

Nicholas, J. (2017, March 30). *10 point checklist for puppy proofing your home.* Preventive Vet. https://www.preventivevet.com/dogs/checklist-for-puppy-proofing-your-home

Ollila, E. (2022, March 9). *Pet safety: Puppy-proofing your home.* Hill's. https://www.hillspet.com/dog-care/new-pet-parent/puppy-proofing-your-home?lightbox fired=true#

Paretts, S. (2022, March 7). *crates for dogs: how to choose the best dog crate.* American Kennel Club. https://www.akc.org/expert-advice/lifestyle/choose-best-crate-dog/

Parks, S., & Coleman, L. (2023, December 22). *Until it clicks: A complete guide to*

clicker training for dogs. The Dog People; Rover. https://www.rover.com/blog/clicker-training-dogs/

Parrish, C. (2020, April 18). *Buying guide: How to choose the best dog crate for your pet*. BeChewy. https://be.chewy.com/dog-crate-buying-guide/

Patience for your puppy or dog. (2023, October 20). Pupford. https://pupford.com/patience-for-your-dog/

Perry, S. (2023, October 18). *New puppy checklist: 9 things you need before bringing home a new upppy*. Be Chewy. https://be.chewy.com/new-puppy-checklist-9-things-you-need-before-bringing-home-a-new-puppy/

Petroff, M. (2022, September 8). *Clicker training dogs: Benefits & tips*. Dutch. https://www.dutch.com/blogs/dogs/clicker-training

Premaza, R. (2023). *Saving Jack: Clicker training an aggressive border collie*. Karen Pryor Clicker Training. https://www.clickertraining.com/node/1650

Pryor, K. (2013a, June 12). *Fifteen tips for getting started with the clicker*. Karen Pryor Clicker Training. https://www.clickertraining.com/15tips

Pryor, K. (2013b, June 12). *Why can't I just use my voice?* Karen Pryor Clicker Training. https://www.clickertraining.com/node/275

Puppy 101: Positive reinforcement dog training. (n.d.). Small Door Veterinary. Retrieved December 22, 2023, from https://www.smalldoorvet.com/learning-center/puppies-kittens/positive-reinforcement-training/

Puppy temperament guide. (n.d.). SnowyPines. Retrieved December 6, 2023, from https://www.snowypineswhitelabs.com/guides/puppy-temperament-guide/

Puppy training that prevents behavioral problems in the future. (2022, January 22). Pet Expertise. https://petexpertise.com/blogs/news/puppy-training-that-prevents-behavioral-problems-in-the-future

Qualtieri, N. (2021, July 1). *Clicker training 101: it really worked for my puppy*. GearJunkie. https://gearjunkie.com/outdoor/hunt-fish/clicker-training-your-dog

Raising puppies has its challenges. (n.d.). Hawthorne Hills Veterinary Hospital. Retrieved November 25, 2023, from https://hhvh.net/2023/04/30/being-a-puppy-parent-can-bring-challenges/

Ramirez, K. (2021). *Thoughts about "the click Is not the trick."* Karen Pryor Clicker Training. https://www.clickertraining.com/thoughts-about-the-click-is-not-the-trick

Randolph, B. (2019, February 6). *Consider your dog's temperament for successful dog Training*. Bow Wow Labs. https://www.bowwowlabs.com/blogs/news/consider-temperament-successful-dog-training

Reisen, J. (2021, April 28). *Bringing a puppy home: help your puppy adjust to a new home.* American Kennel Club. https://www.akc.org/expert-advice/training/8-tips-to-help-your-new-puppy-adjust-to-new-home/

Research Proves your dog jas a unique personality! (2023, January 31). Happy Tails. https://www.happytailsinc.com/research-proves-your-dog-has-a-unique-personality/

Rohats, D. (2016, October 17). *does a dog's personality affect training?* AZ Dog Sports. https://azdogsports.com/does-a-dogs-personality-affect-training/

Sarle, M. J. (2018, April 17). *Keeping a puppy journal.* AKC Pet Insurance. https://www.akcpetinsurance.com/blog/keeping-a-puppy-journal

Schirle, C. (n.d.). *True story: I got a new puppy, and then we both cried all night.* Rover. Retrieved December 12, 2023, from https://www.rover.com/blog/new-puppy-true-story/

Schumer, L. (2019, May 29). *You can teach any dog to behave with these essential commands.* Good Housekeeping. https://www.goodhousekeeping.com/life/pets/g27611300/dog-commands/

The science behind clicker training. (2013, October 13). Faithfully Yours Dog Training. https://fydogtraining.com/training-tips/2015/10/30/the-science-behind-clicker-training

The secret to dog training: Why positive reinforcement works but punishment doesn't. (2021, July 22). Rau Animal Hospital. https://www.rauanimalhospital.com/resources/blog/dogs/secret-dog-training-why-positive-reinforcement-works-punishment-doesnt

Shojai, A. (2019, November 4). *7 Simple steps to clicker training your puppy.* The Spruce Pets. https://www.thesprucepets.com/clicker-training-clicker-train ing-puppy-2805068

Shojai, A. (2023, March 1). *Tests to predict puppy temperament and personality.* The Spruce Pets. https://www.thesprucepets.com/puppy-temperament-testing-2804631

6 Ways to teach your dog basic commands. (n.d.). WikiHow. Retrieved December 17, 2023, from https://www.wikihow.com/Teach-Your-Dog-Basic-Commands

Stordahl, L. (2023, February 13). *6 common clicker training mistakes and misunderstandings.* https://www.thatmutt.com/2014/05/01/6-common-clicker-train ing-mistakes-and-misunderstanings/

Stregowski, J. (2019). *How to solve 10 of the biggest dog behavior problems.* The Spruce Pets. https://www.thesprucepets.com/common-dog-behavior-prob lems-1118278

Stregowski, J. (2021, December 24). *Use these tips to clicker train your dog*. The Spruce Pets. https://www.thesprucepets.com/clicker-training-for-dogs-1118267

Tailor your training to your dog's personality (n.d.). Burgess. Retrieved December 7, 2023, from https://www.burgesspetcare.com/blog/dogs/tailor-your-training-to-your-dogs-personality/

Teach your kids how to treat the new puppy! (2020, September 7). The Puppy Academy. https://www.thepuppyacademy.com/blog/2020/9/7/teach-your-kids-how-to-treat-the-new-puppy

Teaching kids responsibility through dogs (n.d.). Nylabone Dog Toys, Chews, Treats, & Edible Dental Chews. Retrieved December 23, 2023, from https://www.nylabone.com/dog101/teaching-kids-responsibility-through-dogs

32 Wonderful writing about pets prompts (2023, April 10). Journal Buddies. https://www.journalbuddies.com/special-writing-topics/national-pet-day-journal-prompts/

Timing, patience, consistency =3 keys to successful training. (2012, January 31). Advanced Canine Techniques. https://advancedcaninetechniques.com/2012/01/timing-patience-consistency3-keys-to-successful-training/

The top 10 commands to teach your puppy first. (n.d.). Eukanuba. Retrieved December 14, 2023, from https://www.eukanuba.com/au/puppy/puppy-articles/the-top-10-commands-to-teach-your-puppy-first#Lay

Train your dog: The relevance of consistency! (2018, January 8). Tractive. https://tractive.com/blog/en/training-en/consistency-and-rituals-in-dog-training

Training a puppy: A whole family affair. (2023, December 12). Pupford.com. https://pupford.com/training-new-puppy/

Training to your dog's personality. (2012, January 24). DogTime. https://dogtime.com/dog-health/general/369-training-by-personality

21 Common dog training mistakes and how to fix them. (2023, November 14). Pupford.com. https://pupford.com/21-common-dog-training-mistakes/

Van Arendonk, A. (2023). *Carnivorous chairs and the cone of shame: Creativity in Action*. Karen Pryor Clicker Training. https://www.clickertraining.com/node/3978

Welch, W. (2018, February 16). *Positive Reinforcement: Training with treats and praise*. HSHV. https://www.hshv.org/positive-reinforcement-training-dog-cat-treats-praise/

Welcome home, puppy! Introducing your new dog to your other pets. (2011, June 23). DogTails. https://dogtails.dogwatch.com/2011/06/23/welcome-home-

puppy-introducing-your-new-dog-to-your-other-pets/

Welfare of dogs: normal behaviour patterns. (2015, November 19). Nidirect. https://www.nidirect.gov.uk/articles/welfare-dogs-normal-behaviour-patterns

What are a puppy's personality types? (2021, October 19). Petland Texas. https://www.petlandtexas.com/what-are-a-puppys-personality-types/

Why are dog kennel ventilation systems important? (2016, March 30). GUNNER. https://gunner.com/blogs/pack/why-are-dog-kennel-ventilation-systems-important

Why puppies need boundaries! (2020, September 21). The Puppy Academy. https://www.thepuppyacademy.com/blog/2020/9/21/set-boundaries-for-your-puppy

Why the whole family needs to participate in dog training. (2017, January 2). Greg Knows Dogs Blog. https://www.gregknowsdogtraining.com/blog/dog-behaviors/whole-family-needs-participate-dog-training/

Woodnut, J. (2021, February 18). *7 Mistakes people make when training their dogs.* Pawlicy Advisor. https://www.pawlicy.com/blog/dog-training-mistakes/

Made in United States
Orlando, FL
23 May 2024

47139664R10088